ROUTLEDGE LIBRARY EDITIONS:
EXCHANGE RATE ECONOMICS

Volume 11

MODERN FOREIGN EXCHANGE

MODERN FOREIGN EXCHANGE

HUBERT C. WALTER

Routledge
Taylor & Francis Group
LONDON AND NEW YORK

First published in 1923 by Methuen & Co. Ltd.

This edition first published in 2017
by Routledge
2 Park Square, Milton Park, Abingdon, Oxon OX14 4RN

and by Routledge
605 Third Avenue, New York, NY 10017

Routledge is an imprint of the Taylor & Francis Group, an informa business

British Library Cataloguing in Publication Data
A catalogue record for this book is available from the British Library

ISBN: 978-0-415-79325-4 (Set)
ISBN: 978-1-315-21117-6 (Set) (ebk)
ISBN: 978-0-415-79346-9 (Volume 11) (hbk)
ISBN: 978-1-315-21102-2 (Volume 11) (ebk)

MODERN FOREIGN EXCHANGE

BY

HUBERT C. WALTER

M.A., LL.B. (Cantab.); F.I.S.A.

FORMERLY LECTURER IN FOREIGN EXCHANGE TO THE INSTITUTE OF BANKERS, MANCHESTER AND DISTRICT

METHUEN & CO. LTD.

36 ESSEX STREET W.C.

LONDON

First Published in 1923

PRINTED IN GREAT BRITAIN

PREFACE

THIS book on the Foreign Exchanges is founded on lectures delivered from 1919 to 1922 at the Bankers' Institute and at the Municipal School of Commerce of Manchester. The audiences consisted of students preparing for the examinations of the Institute of Bankers, and of business men.

The author's own daily experience of exchange movements and of foreign bills, obtained in his capacity of Financial Manager of a mercantile company trading in various overseas markets, he was enabled to amplify by the facilities kindly afforded him by one of the joint-stock banks for observing the daily work of exchange trading in its foreign branch.

The effects of the war on the economic conditions of Europe are, it is now being recognized, not passing in nature, but in the main destined to be permanent. " Normal " conditions are the conditions not of 1914 but of to-day. The Exchanges of 1922 differ materially from those of pre-war times, and new explanations of their movements have been worked out, associated with the names of Professor Keynes, Professor Cassel, and others. The principles set out in the older textbooks have received extended and sometimes startling applications. Much of the new theory, however, has been written by economists for economists, and is necessarily complicated in form to a degree discouraging to students and business men. It does not seem to have been embodied to any appreciable degree in textbooks. Existing manuals were in the main written with reference to pre-war conditions, and, in so far as they deal at all with modern developments, tend to treat them as temporary aberrations from the "normal." For the ordinary student of Banking, Economics, or Commerce the position is the more unsatisfactory in that he never had experience of financial business under pre-war conditions.

The author has endeavoured to explain the essentials of modern Exchange movements in a form which will be comprehensible to the intelligent person of average education who is not a professional economist. He has had in mind throughout the students and the business men of whom his Manchester audiences were composed. Accordingly, such subjects as inflation, purchasing power parity, the course of the mark and the possibilities of stabilizing the Exchanges and of a return to the gold standard are discussed more fully than has hitherto been the case in textbooks, but in a less technical manner than is necessarily adopted in an economic treatise. The author hopes to find his justification for the book, not in original theories, but in setting out in a form which can be understood by any person of average education the agreed conclusions of economists regarding the post-war Exchanges. The subject of the benefit conferred by a depreciated Exchange on the export trade is examined in rather more detail than seems to have been generally the case hitherto.

Any book on descriptive economics must be part description, part theory: it must aim at describing the phenomena and explaining them. The problem is to balance description and explanation, procedure and theory. In this respect there seemed scope for a book which should combine some of the functions of a banking manual with those of a textbook on this section of economics. Throughout, the author has endeavoured to bear in mind that his readers, like his audiences, will want to know both How? and Why?

In dealing with the procedure relating to foreign bills, the author has drawn on his own experience of both the banking and mercantile aspects. The section on the legal aspect of bills of exchange is not only essential to the understanding of why bills have come to serve as currency, but will also be helpful, it is hoped, to both the student of the law and practice of banking and the young man who is entering on a business career.

In one respect the writing of a textbook on the Foreign Exchanges as they exist to-day presents difficulties unknown to writers before the war. Among the boundaries uprooted by the Governments of Europe is included that between international economics and international politics. In the dangerous No Man's Land now disputed between the two lie such subjects as inflation, the mark, and stabilization. To pass these subjects by would render a book on the modern Exchanges meaningless; to deal with them adequately involves distinguishing between economic considerations and those of a political nature. This distinction the author has carefully endeavoured to observe.

The obligations of the author to existing works are numerous, and have, wherever possible, been acknowledged by footnotes. In particular, it is evident that in dealing with the effect of interest rates on the Exchanges, no textbook can escape heavy obligations to the well-known works of Mr. Withers.

The short bibliography appended will, it is believed, be of assistance to students.

HUBERT C. WALTER

CONTENTS

MODERN FOREIGN EXCHANGE

CHAPTER I

INTRODUCTORY

CURRENCY AND GOLD

Purport of the subject and definitions—Example of exchange transactions—Means of making remittances abroad—Pre-war position of London as a free gold market—Issues involved in remitting money abroad.

IN 1919 the Bankers' Institute altered the syllabus of their examinations by elevating Foreign Exchange into a separate subject. Previously there had only been incidental questions on Foreign Exchange in the papers on the Practice and Law of Banking. The change illustrated the way in which the war had increased the importance of the subject. In 1920 a conference of financial experts representing most of the principal nations in Europe was held at Brussels. The report issued by these experts on existing international commercial and financial conditions centred round the unsettlement of the Exchanges. So much for the importance of exchange matters to the financial community. In the business world the use of the phrase "collapsed exchanges" as indicative of one of the causes of the present trade depression, and of "stabilizing the exchanges" as one of the remedies for that depression, have become commonplaces: before the war both phrases were unknown to the generality of business men.

It is evident that something of a radical nature has happened as a result of the war which has altogether altered the working of the Foreign Exchanges ; and that that alteration is having very far-reaching effects on everyday business life. Perhaps the best example of what the alteration in the exchange position means in practice is this : before the war one pound, when changed into U.S. dollars, would buy 4·86⅔ dollars' worth of wheat. During a great part of 1920 the pound would only buy 3·90 dollars' worth—about 20 per cent. less. That is equivalent to the imposition of a tax of 20 per cent. on wheat imported from the U.S.

The secret of the importance and of the complications of Foreign Exchange to-day is that all the economic forces operating in a country work themselves out in its rate of exchange. The Exchanges register the economic health of a country ; to-day they register the extent to which the economic equilibrium of the world, of Europe especially, has been upset by the war.

Foreign Exchange has one quality about it which makes it both more interesting and more difficult than other sections of economics, in that it deals with economic conditions as they exist from day to day. This makes the subject more difficult, because it means the constant revising of explanations and theories. It also makes it more interesting, because we are enabled to apply our principles to the Exchanges as they exist, and check our theories accordingly.

To clarify our ideas at the outset, we may describe Foreign Exchange as the business of exchanging currencies, or as the study of the ways in which currencies are exchanged ; the Foreign Exchanges are the markets in which this business is done ; and Rates of Exchange are the prices of the various national currencies in terms of other national currencies.

The word " currency " is used in the same sense as

the word " money " is often used. It is necessary to be clear about the meaning of these two terms. " Money " may mean a number of things, " currency " only one. There are certainly four things which the word " money " may mean :

(1) The standard or measure of value.
(2) Medium of exchange.
(3) Purchasing power.
(4) A loan of money.

The last mentioned meaning is the one in which the word is customarily used in the money articles in the newspapers. " Money was cheap to-day " or " Money was dear " obviously does not mean that twenty-one shillings could be obtained for one pound or vice versa. It simply means that if anyone wanted to borrow money, he could do so at a low or high rate of interest. There, clearly, money means " the loan of cash or credit." In the third sense of " purchasing power," an overdraft is money. In neither of these two senses is money equivalent to currency. The first two meanings quoted are in modern practice merged in each other. There is a clear enough theoretical distinction between the standard which measures value and the instrument or medium by which value is transferred from one person to another ; but in the Western European industrial system the monetary system embodies both ideas. In the highly developed commercial system of ancient Babylon, the theoretical distinction was also effective in practice. In a sale of land, the price was agreed in terms of shekel-weights of silver, which were thus the standard of value, but it was paid in corn, slaves, animals, etc., which, valued on the same silver basis, served as the actual media of exchange.[1]

Of these four meanings of the word "money," " currency " is equivalent to the second only, viz. a medium of exchange. Currency means this and only

[1] King : " History of Babylon," pp. 195, 196.

this. It has thus a much more circumscribed meaning than "money," which may have any of the other three meanings indicated. It has, however, a wider meaning than the term "Legal tender," which is that portion of the medium of exchange which a debtor can legally compel his creditor to accept in satisfaction of his debt. Thus an overdraft is money in the sense of purchasing power, but it is not currency. A cheque is currency, but not legal tender. A Treasury note is all three.

The currency of England consists of the following:

(1) Coins.
(2) Treasury notes.
(3) Bank-notes.
(4) Cheques, which are orders to bankers to pay.
(5) Bills of exchange, which are orders to pay.
(6) Interest coupons.

Of the six, the last three are what bankers call "Instruments of Credit," i.e. instruments by which credits, that is to say, book-debts, are recorded and transferred from one person to another. Such is our currency to-day. Before the war it was the same, with the exception that there were no Treasury notes.

The business of exchanging currencies became a necessary part of international trade as soon as international trade developed beyond the stage of barter. When we buy materials abroad, our currency has to be exchanged for the currency of the country in which the seller wishes to be paid, which is generally that of the country in which he is resident. Foreign Exchange is concerned with the quantity of our own currency which we give up in exchange for that of the seller. Assume that "A," a merchant, is trying to sell some mineral that is mined in the United States to a Dutchman. "A" knows he can get £33 per ton c.i.f. Amsterdam for the material. The price we will say is $105 per ton at the American mine. Let us call rail freight $5 per ton and ocean freight \$30 per ton. That gives a total cost to "A" of \$140. Pre-war, when the average rate of exchange with the United States was \$4·86 to the pound, \$140 would represent to "A" in sterling £(140 ÷ 4·86) = £28 16s., i.e. that is the sum which "A" would have had to expend in order to buy \$140 to remit to the exporter. Assuming "A's" gross profit to be 10 per cent., he would require to sell at the price of £31 13s. 7d. In pre-war days Dutch florins could usually be bought at the rate of 12·1 florins to the pound sterling, so that the price of £31 13s. 7d., or, bringing the shillings and pence to decimals of a pound, £31·6794, would represent to prospective Dutch buyers 31·6794 × 12·1 = 383·32 florins. But if the American exchange is what it was frequently during 1919–20—\$3·50 to the pound—then the amount in sterling "A" has to expend in order to purchase \$140 is £(140 ÷ 3·50) = £40. Assuming the same gross profit as before (10 per cent.), "A" will now require to sell at the price of £44. Had the florin been at its usual pre-war rate of 12·1 florins to the pound sterling, this price would have represented to prospective Dutch buyers (44 × 12·1), or 532·4 florins. But at its more usual post-war figure of, say, 11·4 florins to the pound, £44 represents only (44 × 11·4), or 501·4 florins. Even supposing, therefore, that the mineral has remained at exactly the same price as in 1914, the price which "A" can quote to Dutch buyers has been raised from 383·32 to 501·4 florins, solely by the operation of exchange rates. Whether this increase will preclude "A" from continuing to do the business depends, *inter alia*, on whether the florin has become less valuable in terms of the dollar than it was in 1914 to the extent represented by the ratio 501·4 : 383·32. If the florin compared with the dollar has not lost in value to that extent, it will now be more advantageous to the Dutch purchaser to buy direct from New York. It is evident that fluctuations in exchange rates may, quite apart from factors of price, transport, etc., divert the currents of trade or dam them up altogether.

In the example given it will have been noticed that, at different stages of the transaction, " A " had to remit dollars to New York and the Dutch buyer had to remit sterling to London. How can remittances in foreign currency be made ? In pre-war days there would have been five ways :

(1) By sending gold.

(2) By paying out of a foreign currency account.

(3) By sending interest coupons, payable in the foreign currency in question.

(4) By buying from a British bank and sending to the foreign creditor a draft in foreign currency. This draft is drawn by the British bank on a foreign bank situated in the centre in which the creditor resides—Paris, New York, Frankfort, as the case may be—and is for so many francs, dollars, or marks. A variation of this method occurs where the British bank, in return for the payment by the British debtor to it of a sum in sterling or for the authority to debit his account, instructs a bank abroad to pay to the foreign creditor a quantity of foreign currency; such instruction may be by letter (mail transfer), by telegram (telegraphic transfer), or by cable (cable transfer).

(5) By sending the foreign creditor a sterling draft, i.e. a draft entitling him to so many pounds, which he can exchange with his bank for an amount of his own currency.

No. 1 is now impracticable, because prohibited by law ; and pre-war, when it was legal, it was not for obvious reasons resorted to in the ordinary way between merchants. Such sending of gold abroad as occurred was a specialized business in the hands of bullion dealers. But this method of remittance abroad demands a word of mention, for on it depended a vital difference which existed before the war between the currencies of England and the currencies of all other countries. The difference, which no longer exists, was frequently expressed by saying that London was a free market in gold. This meant that anyone who had a claim payable in London could get that claim paid in gold, with the corollary that having got the gold he could do exactly what he liked with it, including the taking of it out of the country. That statement was not always true of any other financial centre in the world. It was generally true in the other big financial centres, but not always, and in that distinction between the words " always " and " generally " lay the ultimate basis of London's pre-war predominance in finance. If a man abroad was owed a debt by a man in London, and told his agent here to collect, the agent could insist on payment in Bank of England notes, and the Bank of England would always change its notes for gold without asking questions or making difficulties. Having obtained the gold, the agent could send it out of the country. That was always true in England up to the end of July, 1914. It was generally true in Berlin, Paris, and New York, but not necessarily. In Paris the Banque de France had the right to redeem its notes in silver, and from time to time it exercised that right. In New York the silver dollar and the silver certificate were legal tender. The rights of the Banque de France to pay its notes in silver and of the American banks to redeem their obligations in silver dollar certificates were used in such a way that people had to be content with silver or silver dollar notes just when they wanted gold most, as in New York at the time of the panic in 1907. In Germany there was no legal bar to the export of gold, and the notes of the Reichsbank were redeemable in gold. But Berlin was not a free market in gold in the same sense as London. On occasion the London-Berlin exchange went to a point at which, according to the theory of exchange, gold was bound to leave Berlin and come to London, because Berlin bullion dealers would have made a profit by sending it, but no gold was allowed to come.[1] This inability to get gold in payment of claims, which occurred on occasion in New York, in Paris and in Berlin, never happened in London before the war. However bad things were, it was always possible to get gold in payment of any claim on a debtor in London. That is the meaning of the phrase that London was a free market in gold. To-day there is in England a legal prohibition on the export of gold, so that the distinction which formerly existed between the currency of England and that of all other countries no longer exists.

Returning now to the other four of the five methods mentioned above whereby remittances abroad may be made, it will be evident that Nos. 2 and 3 are only possible in the special cases where the foreign currency account already exists or the interest coupons happen to be available.

In method No. 4, the most common method of making remittances abroad, the British bank in question has a balance in foreign currency at the foreign bank in question. In handing out a draft on that balance, or instructing the foreign bank to pay part of it away, in exchange for sterling or for the authorization to debit the customer's account, it is exchanging a foreign currency for sterling. The transaction at once raises two questions:

[1] For details of a case in point in 1912, see Withers: "The Meaning of Money," p. 38. The reason why gold did not leave Germany was apparently the opposition to its export by the great German banks—the Deutsche Bank, Dresdner Bank, and Disconto Gesellschaft. The Reichsbank later stated that their opposition had been out of harmony with its own attitude and an error of judgment, and would not be manifested again under similar circumstances. (See Whittaker: "Foreign Exchange," p. 577). The opportunity of testing the correctness of the Reichsbank's forecast passed away in 1914.

How does the bank acquire the currency balance abroad; and at what price will it sell its draft thereon?

In method No. 5 also, where our foreign correspondent exchanges with his bank the sterling draft we sent him for a certain quantity of his own currency, two corresponding questions arise: what use will the buying bank make of the sterling draft, and at what price will it buy?

CHAPTER II

MINT PARS

Gold as an international currency in pre-war days—Resulting stability of rates of exchange—Mint Par—Chain Rule—Table of Currency Units, Mint Pars, and post-war rates.

BEFORE the war, the second of the two questions asked in the last chapter could have been answered approximately at once. There was then never any uncertainty as to what the rates of exchange between the principal European countries and the United States would be, apart from quite minor fluctuations. The rates only moved slightly on one side or the other of a fixed point. The reason for this steadiness was that there existed an international currency. The exchange value of the currencies of the various countries in terms of this common international currency determined their exchange value in terms of each other. This international currency was gold.[1] The use of gold as an international currency determined, within narrow limits, the rates at which currencies were exchanged. The war destroyed this international currency and it is not likely to be reconstituted for an indefinite period. The gold exchange values of most of the currencies are to-day purely theoretical, and offer no guide to the actual rates which obtain. Nevertheless, it is necessary to examine in detail the part which gold played in exchange matters,

[1] This point seems to have first been clearly made by Mr. T. Gregory. See " The Foreign Exchanges, Before, During and After the War."

for the whole of our existing exchange machinery was built up on the assumption that actual rates would deviate only very little from the theoretical gold exchange value. It is because that assumption is no longer true that the machinery, which before the war worked excellently, to-day works unevenly. The understanding of modern conditions of international finance is intimately bound up with a knowledge of their recent history, which has made them what they are. It is necessary to emphasize this, for otherwise the following chapters on Mint Pars and Gold Points, dealing, as they do, with conditions which have in large part passed away, may seem superfluous. But the knowledge contained in them is essential to the understanding of inflation, depreciated exchanges, a return to the gold standard, the importance of the dollar rate, stabilization, etc., in fact, to the understanding of all modern exchange problems.

To begin with, then, the theoretical gold exchange value of a currency is known by the technical term "Mint Par" or "Par of Exchange." The Mint Par or Par of Exchange is the rate at which the standard coin of one country is convertible into that of another country according to the terms of their respective mint laws. The mint laws of the principal countries of the world, apart from the East, prescribe that the standard coin of the country shall, like the sovereign, contain a certain weight of gold, or shall, like the franc, bear a fixed ratio to another coin which contains a certain weight of gold. A comparison of the weight of gold in, or represented by, the two coins, gives an equation showing that the weight of gold represented by a certain number of francs is the same as that contained in a sovereign: in other words, that number of francs equals a sovereign. That equation is called the Mint Par between the two countries.

The Mint Par is therefore a comparison of the value of the units of two currencies on the basis, not primarily of what they will purchase, but of the amount of gold to which their possession entitles the possessor. It is a comparison of gold values.

It follows that, given the terms of the mint laws of any two gold-using countries, it is always possible to ascertain the Mint Par or Par of Exchange between them. The Mint Par between England and France may be taken as an example. The Mint regulations of the two countries are as follow:

(*a*) *England:* 480 troy ozs. of gold, $\frac{11}{12}$ths fine, shall be coined into 1,869 sovereigns.

(*b*) *France:* 1,000 gram. of gold, $\frac{9}{10}$ths fine, shall be coined into 155 napoleons, and one franc is one-twentieth of a napoleon.

We also know (*c*) that 1 oz. troy = 31·1035 gram.

Given the above data, we ascertain the Mint Par by a simple arithmetical operation. Our data we arrange in a set of simple equations, of which number (1) contains the unknown quantity of francs which will be equivalent to a sovereign, number (2) is supplied by (*a*), number (4) by (*c*) and numbers (6) and (7) by (*b*), while numbers (3) and (5) are self-evident arithmetical relations:

(1)	x francs - - -	= 1 sovereign.
(2)	1,869 sovereigns -	= 480 troy oz. standard gold.
(3)	12 troy oz. standard gold - - -	= 11 troy oz. fine gold.
(4)	1 troy oz. fine gold -	= 31·1035 grm. fine gold.
(5)	9 grm. fine gold -	= 10 grm. gold $\frac{9}{10}$ths fine.
(6)	1,000 grm. gold, $\frac{9}{10}$ths fine - - -	= 155 napoleons.
(7)	1 napoleon - -	= 20 francs.

Now the above columns contain two sets of items, of which every one in the left-hand column is equal to a corresponding item in the right-hand column, and vice versa. It follows that if all the items in the first column are multiplied together, the result will be equal to the product of all the items in the second column, thus:

$$x \times 1869 \times 12 \times 1 \times 9 \times 1000 \times 1 = 1 \times 480 \times 11 \times 31{\cdot}1035 \times 10 \times 155 \times 20,$$

whence, $$x = \frac{480 \times 11 \times 31{\cdot}1035 \times 10 \times 155 \times 20}{1869 \times 12 \times 9 \times 1000} = 25{\cdot}2215.$$

The Mint Par between England and France is therefore Fr. 25·2215 = £1.

This operation is—or used to be—known as the "Chain Rule." It simply consists of arranging our data in a number of simple equations, which are set out in such a way that the first denomination is the unknown quantity required, and that the first denomination of every other equation is the same as the second denomination of the equation immediately preceding it. The chain must be continued until it completes itself, i.e. until the second denomination of the last equation is the same as the first denomination of the first equation—in the case above, a certain number of francs. Then, the product of all the quantities in the first column is equal to the product of all the quantities in the second. As there is only one unknown, it can then be found by working out.

Given a knowledge of the mint laws of any two gold-using countries, the Par of Exchange between them can be found by this method.

It will be evident that there can only be a Mint Par between two countries whose standard coins are both gold. If the standard coin of one country is gold, and that of another, such as China, is silver, there can be no Mint Par between them, because there is no fixed relationship between the value of an ounce of gold and the value of an ounce of silver. There is therefore no Mint Par between London and Shanghai.

A further illustration of the meaning of Pars of Exchange is afforded by the following figures:

London/New York Par of Exchange	$4·8665 = £1.
Weight of fine gold in an English sovereign - - -	113·0015 troy gr.
Standard gold according to U.S. mint law - - -	$\frac{9}{10}$ths fine gold.

The first two lines taken together evidently mean that since each is the equivalent of the amount of gold in one gold sovereign, therefore $4·8665 must be the equivalent of 113·0015 grains of gold. Therefore the weight of fine gold in the standard coin of the United States is:

$$\frac{113{\cdot}0015}{4{\cdot}8665} \text{ troy gr.}$$

and the amount of U.S. standard gold in the standard coin must therefore be:

$$\frac{113{\cdot}0015}{4{\cdot}8665} \times \frac{9}{10}$$

or 25·8 troy gr. Such is, in fact, the provision of the American mint law. This does not mean that a gold dollar containing 25·8 troy gr. of gold $\frac{9}{10}$ths fine must be actually minted—in point of fact gold dollars have not been minted since 1890—but that "such gold coins as are struck shall contain this number of grains per dollar of their nominal or legal tender value."[1] Thus the Eagle, one of the gold coins actually minted, has a legal tender-value of $10; hence it must and does contain 25·8 × 10 troy gr. of gold $\frac{9}{10}$ths fine.

There follows a list of the currency of the principal countries of the world, with Mint Pars attached where

[1] Whittaker: "Foreign Exchange."

such exist. The Mint Par rates, it may be repeated, are not only theoretical but were the actual approximate rates which used to obtain before the war.

Centre	Par	Actual Quotation, March 2, 1922	Currency in which Rate is Quoted
Paris	25·22	48·30 — 48·60	Franc and centime
Brussels	Do.	51·15 — 51·32	Do.
Geneva	Do.	22·59 — 22·65	Do.
Belgrade	Do.	350 — 360 (nominal)	Dinar and paras
Athens	Do.	97 — 97⅜	Drachma and lepta
Helsingfors	Do.	217½ — 219	Mark and penni
Madrid	Do.	27·69 — 27·71	Peseta and centimo
Rome	Do.	82⅝ — 83⅝	Lira and centesimi (*Plural* Lire)
Bucharest	Do.	540 — 560	Lev (*Plural* Lei)
Sofia	Do.	640 — —	Leva and statinki
New York	4·867	4·40⅞ — 4·43	Dollar and cent
Montreal	Do.	4·50½ — 4·52	Do.
Berlin	20·43	1,027 —1,074	Mark and pfennig
Amsterdam	12·107	11·57 — 11·58	Florin and cent
Vienna	24·02	23,000 —24,000	Krone and heller (*Plural* Kronen)
Prague	Do.	257 — 262	Do.
Budapest	Do.	2,900 — 3,100	Do.
Warsaw	20·43	17,000 —18,000	Mark and pfennig
Stockholm	18·159	16·71 — 16·74	Krona and öre (*Plural* Kroner)
Kristiania	Do.	25·10 — 25·55	Krone and öre (*Plural* Kroner)
Copenhagen	Do.	20·80 — 20·92	Do.

Of the countries below, France, Switzerland, Belgium, Italy, and Greece are known as "the Latin Monetary Union."

So far, it will be observed we have quoted in every case so many units of foreign currency to one pound. In other cases the style of quoting is different :

Centre	Par	Actual Rates Quoted March 2, 1922	Currency in which Rate is Quoted
Petrograd	94·60	—	Roubles to £10
Lisbon	53·28	$3\frac{9}{32}$ — $3\frac{13}{32}$	Pence per escudo
Rio de Janeiro	16	$7\frac{1}{4}$ — $7\frac{1}{2}$	Pence per milreis
Valparaiso	13·33	38·70—39·40	Pesos to £1
Buenos Aires	47·58	$45\frac{1}{2}$ —$45\frac{3}{4}$	Pence per gold peso
Monte Video	50·98	$44\frac{1}{2}$ —45	Do. dollar
Lima	Par	20°/₀ premium	Eng. £ to Peruvian £
Yokohàmà	$2/0\frac{9}{16}$	$2/1\frac{7}{16}$—$2/1\frac{9}{16}$	Shillings and pence per yen

In the Argentine there is a double currency—the gold peso and the paper peso ; but dealings with foreign countries are almost always conducted in terms of gold pesos or foreign currency.

The following are the chief silver-using centres :

Centre	Rates Quoted March 2, 1922	Currency in which Rate is Quoted
Mexico	2s. 4d.	Shillings and pence per dollar
Alexandria	$97\frac{7}{16}$d.	Piastres to £1
C'nst'ntinople	640—660	Piastres to £1
Shanghai	3s. $0\frac{1}{2}$d.	Shillings and pence to 1 tael
Hongkong	2s. 4d.	Do. Do. 1 dollar
Singapore	2s. $3\frac{11}{16}$d.	Do. Do. 1 dollar

India is a special case of a silver currency based on gold, which will be examined in detail later.

Centre	Par	Actual Rate Quoted on March 2, 1922	Currency in which Rate is Quoted
Calcutta	$\frac{1}{10}$th of £1 (gold)	1s. 3$\frac{3}{16}$d.	Shillings and pence to 1 rupee

The following Central and South American rates are added for the purpose of completeness :—

Country	Mint Par	Actual Rate ruling on Dates Indicated		Currency in which Rates are Quoted
		1922		
Ecuador	10·15	Feb. 25th	16·60	Sucres to £1
Venezuela	25·22	,, 22nd	24·00	Bolivares to £1
Colombia (Bogota)	100·00	,, 28th	99·00	Dollars to £20
Nicaragua	4·87	,, 20th	4·50	Cordobas to £1
San Salvador	9·73	,, 23rd	9·05	Colones to £1
Guatemala	90·23	,, 25th	240·30	Pesos to £1
Costa Rica	10·45	Jan. 28th	18·05	Colones to £1
Bolivia	19·20	,, 21st	14·0	Pence to Bolivano

The currencies of Australia and South Africa consist of Australian and South African pounds, which each contain the same weight of gold as the English pound. The Pars of Exchange would take the form :

£100 (Australian) = £100 (English)
£100 (South African) = £100 (English)

Although these two currencies represent the same weight of gold as the English pound, yet the actual rates at which pounds in England are exchanged for pounds in Australia and South Africa vary just like other rates, for they are subject to the same kind of influences.[1] In the case of Australia, the rate of exchange is quoted

[1] See Chapter VII.

in terms of so many English pounds per Australian £100; thus if the Australian rate be £98½, this means that if you pay to a bank in London £98 10s. they will put £100 to your credit in Sydney. In the case of South Africa, the rate is quoted at so much per cent. premium or discount; thus if South African currency be at a discount of 1½ per cent., you will receive, in return for paying £98 10s. in London, £100 in Johannesburg.

CHAPTER III

GOLD POINTS

In pre-war days fluctuations in exchange rates were limited by Gold Points—Assumptions of the Gold Point theory—Present-day loss of stability—Effect on trading operations—Exchange rates applied in calculating Customs duties.

THE importance of Mint Pars, which represent the theoretical exchange value of one currency in terms of others, based on the amount of gold represented by each, lies in the fact that before the war actual exchange values approximated to these theoretical values very closely, and were bound to do so. The actual Anglo-French rate of exchange, for example, varied above and below 25·22 francs to the extent of a few centimes only. The Foreign exchange machinery which we have was built up on the assumption that the theoretical rates of exchange would be nearly the same as the actual rates. It is because this assumption no longer holds good that the Exchanges are in their present state of disorganization.

Before the war the fluctuations of exchange rates on each side of the Mint Par were not only slight, but definitely limited in extent. The limits were fixed by two points called "Gold Points." These points depended upon the cost of sending gold from one country to another, and were determined respectively by adding that cost to, and subtracting it from, the Mint Par. Thus the Mint Par between London and Paris was 25·22 ; assume that the cost of sending gold in either direction, inclusive of freight, packing, and insurance, was ·07 francs per sovereign; then the gold points were:

25·22 plus ·07 = 25·29 (upper gold point).
25·22 minus ·07 = 25·15 (lower gold point).

The Anglo-French Exchange would ordinarily fluctuate between 25·15 and 25·29, and would not, save in extraordinary cases, move outside those limits.

The statement that the limits within which the rates of exchange would fluctuate were fixed by adding to, and subtracting from, the Mint Par the cost of shipping gold is known as the "Gold Point Theory." As such we shall refer to it; but it is necessary to bear in mind that it was not only a theory, but also a description of what actually happened in practice, subject to certain modifications, which we shall consider later.

Why the cost of shipping gold should fix the limits of exchange fluctuations is not difficult to understand. Suppose "A," an Englishman, having a debt to pay in Paris, went to his bankers and asked them for a draft in francs on Paris. He expected they would sell him a draft on a Parisian bank with whom they kept their balances in francs. The bankers offered to sell him a draft at the rate of 25·14 francs to the pound. "A" would not accept that, because he could send gold more cheaply. The cost of sending gold to Paris, including the charges of the bullion dealer who attended to the shipment, insurance, and freight, was, say, ·07 francs. When the gold arrived at Paris it would realize 25·22 francs for every sovereign. The whole transaction cost "A" seven centimes for every sovereign, so that the nett quantity of francs obtained for every sovereign sent was 25·15. By buying a draft from his banker "A" would have obtained only 25·14 francs. Obviously it was more advantageous to "A" to get 25·15 francs for his sovereign than 25·14 francs. It paid him better therefore to send gold than to buy a draft from his bankers.

Now, assume that "B" in Paris had to pay money in London. His bankers asked, for a draft in sterling, 25·30 francs for every pound. For "B" it was cheaper to send gold. When the gold arrived at London it would realize one pound for every 25·22 francs' worth. It had cost the Frenchman to get the gold over here ·07 francs for every 25·22 francs, so that he had in fact remitted the money to London at the rate of 25·29 francs per pound, which was evidently more advantageous to him than buying a sterling draft at 25·30 francs per pound.

Assuming then, that the cost of sending gold from London to Paris remained constant at 7 centimes per sovereign, gold would be shipped from London to Paris when the rate tended to go below 25·15, and from Paris to London when it tended to go above 25·29. In point of fact, bullion dealers and Foreign Exchange dealers in London and Paris respectively would, when the exchange reached these points, ship gold themselves, and thereby create for themselves balances in the other centre against which they would draw drafts. The fact that this would be done prevented the market rates quoted from going below 25·15 or above 25·29. If the cost of sending gold became less, then the gold points drew a little nearer to one another; if the cost of sending gold became more, then the points moved away from each other. The limits of the fluctuations of exchange were definitely fixed by adding to or subtracting from the Mint Par the cost of shipping gold.

The Gold Point Theory was in the main both a theory and a description of actual fact. There were, however, certain exceptions of detail, relating to both the upper and lower gold points. As regards the lower, gold used on occasion to leave England before, according to the theory, it should have done. The reasons for this are matters of detail which are now of purely historical interest.[1] As regards the upper gold point, rates used on occasion to reach, and pass, the upper gold point without gold coming in. The reason in such a case was that it might be prevented from leaving other countries in the manner explained in Chapter I. London was the only financial centre in the world where no hindrance, legal or practical, was ever placed in the way of the outflow of gold. In Paris and in New York it was on occasion impossible for would-be shippers to obtain gold —the Bank of France exercising its legal right to redeem its notes in silver, the American Treasury utilizing the fact that the silver dollar and silver dollar certificate were legal tender. In Berlin the shipment of gold was apparently prevented for a time in 1912 by official action.[2]

With these modifications the Gold Point Theory held good in practice. That is what is meant by the statement that before the war international indebtedness could always be settled by the shipment of gold. That is not of course to say that the exchanges were normally corrected by this means. Normally, indeed, before the war, the corrective to exchange movements was supplied by the ordinary processes of trade[3] or by the manipulation of discount rates.[4] The operation of these two factors we shall discuss in detail later. The importance of shipments of gold lay in this, that where trade processes or manipulation of discount rates failed to correct the fluctuations of the exchanges, shipments of gold were always a possibility in reserve. They were not normally required in order to fix the exchanges between the gold

[1] They are examined in detail in Withers' "Money Changing," pp. 161–2.

[2] See footnote, p. 8.

[3] Examined in Chapters VII and VIII.

[4] Examined in Chapter X.

points, but where the two factors named were not adequate to effect this, there was always the possibility of shipping gold, and that possibility was used on a number of occasions. The exchanges before the war never reached a point at which the rates were too far from the Mint Par to be corrected by the shipment of gold.

The question naturally arises: Why this insistence on gold? The experience of generations has established that gold is in practice the best available basis for currency. One reason for this is that gold, while by no means absolutely stable in value, is stable relatively to the fluctuations in value of other commodities. The supply cannot be suddenly increased or diminished. In this respect it stands in the greatest contrast to paper money, which can be printed *ad infinitum* by any government. A gold basis to a currency, again, is a far simpler arrangement than would be the basing of currency on the exchange value of wheat or other commodities. In any case, on whichever side the balance of theoretical advantage may be, the fact remains that before the war the gold basis worked very well by reason of the fact that everywhere in the world people do, as a matter of fact, want gold. Everywhere in the civilized world people will, as a matter of fact, take gold under any circumstances. A man in New York with a bag of sovereigns can always go to the U.S. Treasury and get them changed for dollars at the par rate. When sterling drafts were being sold for $3·90 a man with sovereigns in New York could always get $4·8665 for each sovereign. Some people have made it their business to attack this preference for gold as unreasonable. It may be. It may be a fact, as Mr. Hartley Withers, himself a believer in the advantages of the gold standard, has suggested that people only want gold because every one else wants it. However that may be, the preference itself, and with it the fact that the volume of gold in existence cannot be suddenly increased, were facts sufficiently strong to have induced all the principal commercial countries of Europe and America before the war to adopt the gold basis. Gold thereby became an international currency, and the assumption became justified that a country's currency was a claim to so much gold, and that that claim could if desired be enforced. In other words, if an Englishman had a draft payable in Berlin or Frankfort in marks, or in Paris in francs, that draft represented a claim to so much gold from Germany or France as the case might be. If a Frenchman had a draft payable in London in sterling, that draft represented a claim to so much gold from England. In either case the claim could be enforced if desired. That assumption underlay the Gold Point Theory. On that assumption the whole exchange machinery of the world was built.

Neither part of the assumption is true to-day. Two entirely different conditions have come into existence as a result of the war. The first is that each of the belligerent countries, with the exception of the United States, has issued an amount of paper currency far in excess of its gold cover. Such large masses of paper money have been issued that the possession of these currencies cannot in practice entitle the possessor to the equivalent in gold —there is not enough gold to cover the amount of currency issued. The process has gone to its extreme extent in Russia, Poland, and Austria, and in Germany. In England also paper money has been over-issued. The second condition brought about by the war, which renders untrue the second part of the assumption—that the claim to gold can be enforced—is that in every one of the principal countries of the world, except the United States, there exists a legal prohibition on the export of gold.

It follows that even in England, and still more on the

continent of Europe, the assumptions on which the Gold Point Theory was based no longer hold true.

The effect of these conditions can be put in another way by saying that the currencies of the world, again bar that of the United States, have lost their intrinsic value, that is, the value which before the war they possessed in themselves by virtue of being a claim to so much gold. Currency always had value in the sense that it was purchasing power. If a man had so many marks at his disposal, they always had value in the sense that if he went into a shop in Berlin he could buy a certain quantity of goods. But apart from that, these marks had a value in themselves because they represented so much gold. That is what is meant by intrinsic value.

To-day they do not represent any gold; they merely retain their first quality of purchasing power.

In losing intrinsic value the currencies have also lost stability, because their value, being merely what they can purchase, fluctuates from day to day. At a time when prices are rising or falling rapidly, owing to alterations in the price of raw material, wages, etc., the value of a currency which represents solely purchasing power fluctuates accordingly. Currency to-day, outside the U.S., has come to represent merely a right to a fluctuating quantity of the produce of the country in question, and nothing more. The extreme case of this is seen in Eastern Europe, where the ability to produce at all has almost been lost, as in Russia, and the currency has lost value altogether.

Having lost the gold basis, and with it intrinsic value and stability, the currencies of the world, with the exception of the dollar, are at the mercy of market conditions. A general view of what this means is obtained by comparing the second and third columns in the European section of the table given in Chapter II.

The second column gives the par rates of exchange, which before the war were very nearly the actual rates; column three indicates the amounts of the European currencies which in the spring of 1922 had to be given up in exchange for the pound. The loss in value is striking; even more so are the fluctuations from week to week and from day to day. Since the table was compiled the position has become worse, as a glance at the money article in a daily newspaper will show.

What the loss of stability in currency values means in practice can easily be seen. Assume that a German importer buys a quantity of raw material through a London merchant, and has to pay in sterling. The price, let us say, is £240, payable by a three months' bill. The rate of exchange at the time the purchase is made is Mk. 800. The cost of raw material he accordingly reckons at Mk. 240 × 800 = Mk. 192,000, which sum he will have to pay at the end of three months. Assuming that the work put into the raw material costs him, including all charges, an amount equal to the cost of raw material, then his final cost will be Mk. 192,000 × 2 = Mk. 384,000. If he contents himself with 5 per cent. profit, his selling price will be Mk. 403,200. By the time the bill is due, however, the value of the mark has fallen, and the rate is no longer 800 but 1,200. The transaction then appears as follows:

Marks required to pay bill of £240 = 240 × 1200 Mk. - - -	= Mk. 288,000
Marks expended in labour and charges	192,000
Total Cost - - - -	480,000
Sale Price - - - -	403,200
Loss - -	Mk. 76,800

In other words, a perfectly sound business transaction has been turned into a loss by the mere operation of exchange forces over which the importer had no control. It can easily be understood how under these conditions the most legitimate trade may become nothing more than a gamble.

In view of the course of the mark in the autumn of 1921 and summer of 1922 the fluctuation assumed above is a very moderate one—no more, in fact, than actually happened on occasion during a single week-end.

In one direction the depreciation and fluctuation of the exchanges which have been characteristic of the post-war period has led to particularly interesting and unexpected results. This is in the calculation of customs duties. It clearly makes a great difference, when duties are being calculated on the foreign currency in which the invoice is made out, whether that currency is converted at the par value or at the exchange of the day. The following quotation from the " Bulletin of the Federation of British Industries " dated September 27th, 1921, which deals with the position in New Zealand, puts the issue very clearly:

" Take an article whose value in British currency is £100 and on which the British preferential tariff is 20 per cent., and the general tariff 30 per cent. The duty on this article, if imported from Great Britain, is at present levied by the New Zealand Customs authorities on the U.K. price, i.e. £100 plus a charge of 10 per cent. made by the Customs to cover the cost of freight, packing, and insurance. The total sum on which duty is payable is therefore £110, which at 20 per cent. equals £22 duty.

" A similar article is worth in the United States about $389 (at an average exchange rate of $3·89 = £1). It might be expected that on the 30 per cent. basis for non-British goods the duty on the American article would amount to £33. What actually happens is that the cost price of $389 is converted at the Mint Par of exchange of 4·86 = £1. This gives an equivalent in British currency of only £80, or £88 with the additional 10 per cent. duty. Calculated on this sum the duty payable at 30 per cent. amounts to £26 8s. Instead, therefore, of the British article receiving a full 10 per cent. preference, the actual preference is only about 4 per cent.

"It is a matter for congratulation that a cable was received on September 19th by the High Commissioner for New Zealand in London, stating that as from the beginning of next year this method of assessing duty would be discarded. Instead, the New Zealand Customs authorities will assess the duty to be paid on goods imported from countries with an appreciated currency on the bank or current rate of exchange. This means that the British manufacturer will secure the full preference granted to him by the New Zealand Customs tariff."

It is evident that if the par rates are taken as the basis of calculation, countries with a depreciated rate of exchange are penalized in comparison with countries whose rates have not depreciated, or not depreciated to so great an extent. In the case of Australian duties, French, Italian, and Belgian exporters were protesting in 1919 against the use of par rates. These rates placed them at a disadvantage against British competitors for precisely the same reason that, in the case of New Zealand taken up by the F.B.I., British exporters were placed at a disadvantage with American. In the case of Australia, however, the British exporters' interest was the same as that of the American exporter in the case of New Zealand: he was competing against exports sold in depreciated currencies. In the case of Australia, therefore, the British exporter used the argument that if the duty were calculated at current rates of exchange, countries with a depreciated currency would enjoy an unfair advantage, because a pound would purchase more in those countries than in Britain. This last assumption, however, is by no means always true. When and how far it is true depends on the extent to which home prices have approximated to world prices; and this in turn depends on whether the depreciated currency is steady at its low level or is still in a state of fluctuation.[1] It would appear that if the currencies of the principal countries remain steady at some new level, home and world prices will tend to approximate, in which case the fairer way of calculating customs duties is on the basis now adopted by New Zealand, i.e. taking current rates of exchange. So long, however, as considerable fluctuations occur, hardship to somebody is inevitable, whichever method is adopted.

[1] This subject is dealt with in Chapter XII.

CHAPTER IV

BILLS OF EXCHANGE

How foreign currency balances are acquired—Bills of exchange —Example—Legal definition—Rights and liabilities of parties—Why bills serve as currency—Foreign bills—Example—Relation of foreign bills and their prices to exports and imports—London's international acceptance business—Summary of conclusions. Appendix: specimen letter of lien.

WE have seen that as the Gold Point Theory of the exchanges no longer applies, it is nowadays not possible to say immediately at what approximate price the holder of a foreign currency balance will sell it. We must examine in detail at what price he could replace it. This is equivalent to answering the first of the two questions asked at the end of Chapter I.: how he acquired the balance. How, in other words, do foreign currency balances come into existence?

Starting from the beginning, we may take the case where the foreign department of the Manchester office of one of the joint-stock banks sells to a customer a draft on a foreign country—let us say a draft in kroner on a bank in Stockholm. A number of customers will come in and ask for such drafts, and the bank's balance in Swedish kroner in Stockholm will become exhausted unless replenished. To replenish that balance the branch applies to its head office in London. The London office buys the necessary kroner from a foreign exchange broker who specializes in Swedish exchange. But that only removes the question further back. How does the broker get possession of the kroner ? The answer is, in outline, that thes broker buys debts owing by Swedes to English merchants, and sells them to the foreign department of the head office. These debts are in the form of bills of exchange. What the broker does is to buy bills of exchange draw on, i.e. payable by, people in Stockholm, and sell them to the head office of the bank. The price at which the broker sells will ultimately be determined by the price at which he can buy ; the price at which he can buy will be determined by the demand and the quantities there are on offer. The price at which he sells to the London bank will determine the price at which the head office of that bank will sell the kroner to its branches, and that in turn will determine the price at which the branches will sell kroner to their customers who want drafts. Ultimately, therefore, the price at which a draft on Stockholm can be sold depends upon the price at which the bills of exchange on Stockholm can be bought. It is bills of exchange which provide the funds on which foreign drafts are drawn. The international indebtedness with which foreign exchange deals is made up of claims which in the main take the form of, or are settled by the remittance of, bills. The price of a foreign currency is the price of bills drawn on that foreign centre. It goes to the very core of the subject, therefore, to examine bills in detail. What are bills of exchange and how do they originate ?

Suppose H.C.W. & Co., Ltd., are merchants importing timber from the Baltic provinces. They have to pay fairly prompt cash for the timber they import. Their customers are, in the main, builders, notoriously slow payers. H.C.W. & Co., Ltd., will in a number of cases draw bills on them, which take the form of orders to them to pay at a certain time.

The bill of exchange is in the following form :

No....... £100 0s. 0d. Date......
At ninety days' date pay to our order the sum of one hundred pounds. Value received.

For and on behalf of
H.C.W. & Co., Ltd.,
To Messrs. A. & B., Ltd., T. Brown, Secretary.
Salisbury.

This document, with invoice and delivery note for the timber, is sent to Messrs. A. & B., Ltd., or the documents may be presented through a bank. A. & B. keep the delivery note and get the timber, and return the bill, having written across the face of it :

Accepted. Date...... Payable at Barclays Bank, Salisbury.
For and on behalf of A. & B., Ltd.,
J. Jones, Secretary.

H.C.W. & Co., Ltd., can now sell this document to a bank for cash, with which they can pay for the timber imported. The price the banker will pay for it will be something less than the face value of £100 ; it will be £100 less interest for the period the bill has to run calculated at the rate obtaining for that class of bill. Ninety-three days after the date of the bill the then holders of the bill will present it to Barclays Bank, Salisbury, who will pay it and debit the A. & B. Co.'s account.

In this case the bill was in the first instance merely evidence of a debt which A. & B. owe H.C.W. & Co. ; when sold to the banker it became an Instrument of Credit, a means, i.e. whereby A. & B.'s debt was transferred from H.C.W. & Co., Ltd. to the banker. The banker who has bought it may in turn sell it to a broker, he to a fourth buyer. In thus going from hand to hand it is serving as currency in the same way as a Treasury note.

These bills of exchange have been well-known commercial instruments since the fourteenth century. They were developed first among the Italian commercial community in Florence, where banking originated. From Italy they spread through the commercial cities of Germany—the Rhineland towns and the Hansa League—to England. During the following centuries they came more and more into use among merchants, but the rights and obligations of the parties to them were not recognized by the common law. Such was the position at the beginning of the nineteenth century. The law is built up largely on decided cases. During the first quarter of the nineteenth century a large body of commercial customs, which previously had not had the force of law, became incorporated into the English common law through the decisions of a number of Lord Chancellors, more particularly of Lord Eldon; and among such commercial customs were a number relating to bills of exchange. From time to time conflicting decisions were given, which created difficulties for the commercial community. Towards the end of the century a portion of the commercial law of this country was codified, one portion so treated being the whole of the law relating to bills of exchange and cheques, which is now to be found in the Bills of Exchange Act of 1882.

By that Act a bill of exchange is defined as "an unconditional order in writing, addressed by one person to another, signed by the person giving it, requiring the person to whom it is addressed to pay on demand or at a fixed determinable future time a certain sum in money to or to the order of a specified person or to bearer."[1] In other words, it is an order from "A" to "B" to pay a certain sum at a determinable time to "A" or to "C." The amount and the time must both be definite.

The following details regarding the form in which bills

[1] Section 3 (1).

are drawn, and the rights and liabilities of parties to them, are material.

In the example quoted, H.C.W. & Co., Ltd., are the drawers of the bill, and A. & B., Ltd., are the drawees. As the bill is payable to the order of H.C.W. & Co., Ltd., the latter are also the payees, but the payees might equally well have been a third party, such as a bank, who were collecting the bill on behalf of H.C.W. & Co., Ltd. In the case given when A. & B., Ltd. promised to pay, or, in other words "accepted," the bill by writing that word across the face of it, they became acceptors. Save in exceptional circumstances, a bill can only be accepted by the drawee. The acceptance, again, might simply have read :

Accepted.
For and on behalf of A. & B., Ltd.,
J. Jones, Secretary.

Such an acceptance is known as an "Acceptance in Blank."

There is one other party to a bill who requires mention, and that is the endorser. When "X" sells a bill, accepted by "K," "X" will write his name on the back, thereby becoming an endorser. The acceptor "K" is primarily liable on the bill, but if "K" fails to pay the bill when it is due, the holder can sue either "K," or "X" (or any other endorser), or the drawer. If the holder recovers from "X," "X" in turn can recover from any previous endorser, or from "K," or from the drawer.

A bill may be drawn at sight, in which case it has to be paid as soon as it is presented, and is known as a "Sight Draft." Bills may also be drawn at 8, 30, 60, or 90 days' sight or date, or longer. If the bill is claused "At thirty days' sight pay . . .," the period runs from the date when the bill was sighted, i.e. presented for acceptance; if it is claused "At thirty days' date pay . . .," the period runs from the date of the bill itself, irrespective of when it was sighted. In the case of both bills drawn at so many days' sight and so many days' date the period is increased by three days of grace, so that a bill at 30 days' sight is in fact payable 33 days after sight, a bill at 60 days' date at 63 days after date. But the date must be a definite, ascertained date; not some indetermined time, such as "when delivery of the goods is made." The date on which a bill becomes due for payment is known as "maturity."

If a bill is payable on demand by a banker it is called a cheque; if it is payable forthwith or at any future time by anyone else than a banker, or payable in the future by a banker, it is a bill of exchange in the ordinary sense. In other words, the phrase "Bill of Exchange" is a little vague in meaning. Legally it means all documents which come within the definition quoted above.[1] In practice, we abstract a certain class of such documents and call them "cheques." The class so abstracted consists of those bills which are payable by a banker on demand. This is equivalent to saying a cheque is a sight draft drawn on a banker. The money columns of the newspapers, however, frequently use the term "cheque" for any sight draft: thus the term "the Paris cheque" means a sight draft on Paris.

A sight draft has only a 2d. stamp, whereas a bill of exchange of any other kind has to be stamped *ad valorem*, at the following rates:

Up to £75 - - -	9d.
£75 to £100 - - -	1s.
£100 to £200 - - -	2s.,
etc., etc.	

Two other terms should be noted: "Trade Paper" and "Bank Paper." Trade paper consists of bills

[1] See p. 33.

accepted by merchants. Bank paper means bills accepted by banking institutions. The words "banking institution" is used advisedly to indicate not merely the joint-stock banks, but any of the merchant banks or accepting houses. A merchant bank or accepting house is a banking institution which specializes in commercial credit operations. It receives commission for lending its credit. It does this by allowing approved clients, usually merchants, to draw bills on it up to a specified amount, not relating to any particular shipment of goods, and sometimes not to any goods at all. The merchant who draws such drafts discounts them with his own bank and thus provides himself with ready cash. When drawing he obligates himself to put the accepting house in funds to meet the draft 48 hours before it is due for acceptance. He pays the acceptors a commission ($\frac{3}{8}$ per cent. to $\frac{5}{8}$ per cent.) immediately the draft is returned to him accepted, and also pays the acceptors' expenses in respect of postage. By the time the bill matures—such drafts are usually of two or three months' maturity—the merchant has received the payments he was anticipating and remits the value of the draft to the accepting house 48 hours before it is due to be presented to the latter for payment. A draft not relating to any goods at all is known as a "Finance Bill," as opposed to a "Commercial Bill," and the drawer is said to be drawing against a blank credit. For some time past the Bank of England is understood to have expressed some doubt as to the wisdom of giving blank credits, and a new form of bill has come into existence which is a hybrid between a commercial bill, which relates to a shipment of goods, and a finance bill proper, which is drawn under a blank credit and does not relate to any goods at all. This hybrid bill is drawn against a blank credit, as is the finance bill proper, but is secured by the merchant giving to the accepting house a general lien on all his shipments, or on all his shipments to a particular market,[1] and on the proceeds arising therefrom, which proceeds he agrees to place in a separate account earmarked for the purpose of repaying the loan from the acceptors. Under these arrangements between merchants and accepting houses it is frequently provided that a merchant is at liberty to draw up to a certain amount, say £10,000, and that when any part of the £10,000 is repaid by him he may immediately draw that amount again, thereby bringing up the total of the advances to him to £10,000 again. A continuing credit of this kind is known as a "revolving credit."

Such being the general character and the uses of bills of exchange, we have now to examine how it is that these documents can serve, not merely as evidence of debts and as instruments of credit, but as currency. They are enabled to do this by the possession of certain legal characteristics which make bills of exchange documents of a class known as "negotiable instruments." The chief of these characteristics of bills of exchange are two :

(*a*) They are transferable by delivery.

(*b*) Delivery gives a good title.

The quality of being transferable by delivery may be thus explained. If a person is selling shares, he has to sell them by means of a document in a particular form, known as a "Transfer." Unless the sale is made by means of a transfer it is not valid. In the case of a bill of exchange no such document is needed. A good legal sale is effected by "A" handing to "B" the money, and "B" endorsing the bill and handing it to "A." That is known as "delivery," and delivery alone effects a sale. There is no need for a transfer form such as is necessary in the case of a share certificate.

As regards (*b*), "Delivery gives a good title." Suppose

[1] A specimen letter of Lien is given in Appendix to this Chapter.

" A " loses a watch, " B " finds it and sells it to " C." " C " does not know that " B " is not the owner of the watch, and pays a fair price for it. It comes to " A's " knowledge that " C " has his watch. " A " can compel " C " to return it to him. " A " could sue " C " if necessary and the Court would give " A " the watch. " C " has no good title to the watch, although he bought it *bona fide* and for value. Now suppose " A " has a bill of exchange which " B " steals and sells to " C." " C " does not know that " B " has got the bill wrongly, and buys it in good faith, paying a good price for it. " A " has no right of action against " C." " C " has a good title to the bill as against " A." Although " B " himself had no title to the bill, he can give a title to " C." A party in " C's " position who has bought the bill of exchange for value, and *bona fide*, unaware that " B " had no good title to the bill, is called the " Holder in Due Course."

To be a Negotiable Instrument a document must possess both characteristics (*a*) and (*b*), as does e.g. a banknote or Treasury note. A bill of lading is (*a*) transferable by delivery, like a bill of exchange; but it is not (*b*) capable of acquiring a good title by delivery, and therefore it is not a negotiable instrument. The ordinary cheque, which is simply a particular form of a bill of exchange, possesses (*a*) and (*b*) and is therefore negotiable. The effect of crossing a cheque " not negotiable " does not, and is not intended to, prevent or restrict transfer of the cheque by ordinary endorsement; the effect of such crossing is that the person receiving the cheque gets no better title than had the person from whom he obtains it. Crossing a cheque " not negotiable," in other words, leaves characteristic (*a*) untouched but destroys (*b*).

The bill of exchange owes its ability to serve as currency first to its legal character as a negotiable instrument, and secondly to its common commercial use. A Foreign Bond transferable by delivery is equally a negotiable instrument, but it does not serve as currency, because it does not possess the commercial popularity of the bill of exchange.

Bills of exchange serve as currency by being transferred from one person to another by sale, a process which is known as "discounting" or "negotiating." When H.C.W. & Co., Ltd., negotiated the bill accepted by the A. & B. Co., Ltd., with H.C.W. & Co.'s bankers, the latter, we saw, paid the H.C.W. & Co., Ltd., a price which was the face value of the bill less an amount representing interest for the period the bill had to run. The interest is known as discount. The price of a bill is quoted in terms of the rate of discount which will be deducted from it. In this case it was a three months' bill, and on the particular date in question three months' Trade Bills were quoted in the Press at, say, $5\frac{1}{2}$ per cent. A "Trade Bill" is one which, like the bill under discussion, is drawn on and accepted by a trading firm, that is, any firm not a bank. The quotation means that trade bills which have three months to run can be sold at a price which is arrived at by deducting interest at $5\frac{1}{2}$ per cent. for the period which the bill has to run. The amount therefore which the H.C.W. & Co., Ltd., will get for their bill of £100 is arrived at as follows:

$$
\begin{aligned}
\text{£100 minus } \frac{100 \times 11 \times 1}{100 \times 2 \times 4} &= \text{£100 minus } 1\tfrac{3}{8} \\
&= \text{£100 minus £1 7s. 6d.} \\
&= \text{£98 12s. 6d.}
\end{aligned}
$$

The specimen bill set out above was an inland bill. A foreign bill is one drawn or payable in a foreign centre. It is with foreign bills that we are mainly concerned. They are more complicated than inland bills, and the procedure followed in dealing with them is varied. At a later stage we shall have to deal with foreign bills exhaustively, but here we are only concerned with their use as currency and their function in building up foreign currency balances on which banks can draw drafts. We will therefore examine, in outline only, two ways in which foreign bills come into existence and create foreign balances, remembering meantime that there are alternative ways of dealing with them to those we are assuming.

Suppose " X " is a firm exporting structional steelwork to Swedish contractors known as Franssons. " X " has an agent in Stockholm. " X " ships the steelwork and sends the invoice and shipping documents to his agent, together with a 60 days' draft on Franssons for 1,000 kr. The agent gets Franssons' acceptance of the draft and thereupon hands them the shipping documents giving control of the goods. The accepted bill, we will assume, is returned to " X " in about ten days. A bill-broker, i.e. a dealer in bills, who specializes in Swedish Exchange, buys the draft from " X " and sells it to the Foreign Department of a London bank. The latter send it to their Swedish correspondents to await maturity, when it will be paid and credited to the London bank's account. From the time when the bank buys the draft, it is in a position to draw drafts on its Swedish correspondents of such a maturity that they will fall due for payment coincidently with the crediting of their account with the proceeds of the draft on Franssons. Or the Swedish correspondents might be requested to discount the draft themselves and place the proceeds to the credit of the London bank's account, and do so, whereupon the London bank would be able to draw sight drafts at once.

The bill might be dealt with in another way. The agent having got it accepted might sell it to a Swedish bank, and remit to " X " that bank's draft in kroner.

In that case " X " could sell the kroner draft to the bill-broker, and the same result is achieved.

Yet another possibility is that " X " might send the draft for collection. In that case " X " would take it to his own bank and ask them to collect. His bank would send the draft and documents with it to their branch or correspondents in Stockholm. The latter would present the draft for acceptance, and when it was accepted would hand over the documents just as the agent had done. When the draft matured, in one or two months, they would present it again for payment. When it was paid they would advise and credit " X's " bank here and the latter would credit " X " with the equivalent in sterling. " X's " bank now has a balance in kroner in Stockholm, and can draw on that kroner balance which it acquired by collecting " X's " bill, and sell the drafts once again to our bill-broker.

The bill drawn on Franssons has thus illustrated how a foreign bill operates to replenish the kroner balances of a British bank.

Had the bill been drawn, not in kroner, but in sterling, the question would have arisen, when Franssons paid: At what rate would they pay kroner for each pound of the face value of the bill? That question we must leave until later.[1] The point we are concerned with is that Franssons would have had to pay kroner, so that whether the draft is drawn in sterling or kroner it would have the same effect of putting a bank here in possession of a kroner balance in Stockholm, against which they can issue drafts; and that it would be at their own discretion whether such drafts were issued at sight or at so many days' date or sight.

The example given is the sort of thing which, in general outline, is happening every day. Every day there are drafts moving about for different amounts, in different

[1] See Chapter VI.

currencies, on different financial centres, and maturing at different dates. The bill-broker buys the drafts he knows the banks will want, and sells to the banks which want them. The price at which the bill-broker sells the drafts to the banks will determine the price at which the Foreign Department of the banks will sell to their branches, and that price will in turn determine the price at which the branches will sell to their customers. The price at which the bill-broker sells will in turn be determined by the price at which he can buy. Therefore the price at which drafts on a foreign centre can be sold to customers at any given time will be determined by the price at which bills on that centre can be bought. That price in turn will depend on the supply of and the demand for bills, actual and anticipated.

As to the supply, it is evident from the above example that bills on Stockholm will come into existence as a result of exports to Sweden. The more goods we export to Sweden the bigger will be the kroner balance on which banks here can draw, and assuming that the demand for kroner remains the same, there will be more kroner available than there would have been if " X " and other merchants had not sold goods to Sweden, and thereby created the balance. The demand for kroner being unaltered, and the supply having increased, the value will go down. In other words, buyers of kroner will get more kroner for every pound than they got before. The exchange rate will go up: the value of sterling, in terms of kroner, has increased. We come to the conclusion that, all other things being equal, exports will send up the value of a country's currency.

Now as to the demand for bills on Stockholm. Suppose " Y " to be a merchant importing paper. " Y " will want to buy kroner drafts to pay for his imports. Every shipment of paper to this country will give rise to a demand from " Y " and similar merchants, or from their banks, for kroner bills, with which to replenish their Swedish balances. Assuming the supply of kroner remains unaltered, and this increased demand, the value of kroner will go up. For every pound " Y " or his bank will get less kroner than previously. The exchange rate will go down : the value of sterling, in terms of kroner, has declined. Therefore, other things being equal, a surplus of imports over exports will tend to diminish the value of a country's currency, just as a surplus of exports over imports will tend to increase it.

The bill on Stockholm came into existence as the result of the export of goods to Sweden, and the bill on London as the result of the import of goods into England. But bills on London may come into existence as the result of the shipment of goods from one part of the world direct to another without coming to England. London in effect pays for, or guarantees the payment for, the goods to the seller and collects the price from the buyer, plus a commission for the trouble and the responsibility taken. London finances international trade and takes a tribute therefrom for doing so, and the process brings bills on London into existence and creates a corresponding demand for sterling. An example will make this clear.

A Chinaman, Chung Ling Soo, in Canton, exports tea. An Italian merchant, Valentini, in Milan, imports tea. Valentini wishes to place a contract with Chung Ling Soo for tea. Chung Ling Soo is willing to sell to Valentini, provided terms of payment can be arranged to mutual satisfaction, the difficulty being that while both persons are of undoubted financial rectitude, they are unknown to each other, and therefore not prepared to trust each other. Valentini does not wish to pay for the tea until it arrives at the Italian port, and Chung Ling Soo does not want to ship the tea until he is paid, or knows for certain that he will be paid. The gulf is bridged by an accepting house. Steinfelds are, let us say, an accepting house in London. Their business is lending their credit for a consideration. What they do in this case is to agree to pay the bills for Valentini up to a certain amount, the consideration being that Valentini is to put them in funds to the amount of the bills at least 48 hours before they mature in London, and to pay them a commission for taking the responsibility as against Chung Ling Soo. Steinfelds, therefore, get a commission and two days' interest on the money of someone else, and that without the outlay of a penny. Steinfelds inform the London office or agents of the Canton Bank that they (Steinfelds) will accept bills drawn by Chung Ling Soo on themselves, at, let us say, 60 days, covering the shipment of tea to Valentini at a certain price. Steinfelds take the risk which Chung Ling Soo will not take, because Chung Ling Soo is simply a tea merchant, while Steinfelds are an accepting house, and it is part of their business to know on behalf of whom they can safely accept bills, and on behalf of whom they cannot. Chung Ling Soo on his part is quite prepared to take Steinfeld's assurance of payment, where he would not take Valentini's, because, as a merchant, he knows the repute of Steinfelds.

Chung Ling Soo ships the tea, and draws on Steinfelds. He presents the bill on Steinfelds together with documents covering the shipment to the Canton Bank, and the Canton manager of that bank is ready to advance him money on the bill drawn on Steinfelds although it is not yet accepted, because Steinfelds have promised that they will accept. Steinfelds' reputation is such that the promise is good enough for the manager in Canton. He sends the bill, together with documents, to his head office in London. The London office present to Steinfelds, Steinfelds accept, and when it falls due 60 days after sight they pay. In return for accepting they get the documents covering the tea, which is now on its way. How Steinfelds deal with the documents is a matter of detail. Valentini may be an old and valued client, and they may be willing to send him the documents straight away and simply ask him to remit before the draft matures. His remittance will most likely take the form of a sight draft on a London banker, which he will buy from his banker. It may be that they will draw on Valentini, and send their draft, with the documents covering the tea, to a bank in Milan, the documents to be handed over against acceptance or against payment of their draft. The important point is that they send the documents to him and he pays them, either by buying a bill on London, or by paying their draft on him, at least 48 hours before the draft on him matures.

In this transaction there is first the coming into existence of a bill on London and then the buying of a bill on London or alternately the drawing of a bill on Milan. Chung Ling Soo drew on Steinfelds; Valentini, in order to meet his financial obligations, buys a bill on London or accepted one on himself. Both these operations have arisen out of a shipment of tea from Canton to Milan, which does not come to England at all.

Balancing the transaction, it is evident that London has paid away so much and has got in rather more, the difference being represented by Steinfelds' commission and the 48 hours' interest. That is an example of how London finances world trade, and takes a commission for doing so, the process being operated by two bills, one on London and one on Milan. The whole operation clearly hinges on the willingness of Chung Ling Soo to accept without question payment by a bill on London. That willingness originated in the fact that before the war a bill on London was the safest form of international currency, because it was the equivalent to a claim to so much gold.

Its value, in terms of other currencies, could not vary

beyond the minute fluctuations which brought it to the gold points. To-day[1] a bill on New York from a purely currency point of view would be better, because a bill on New York is still a claim to gold and a bill on London is not. In fact, the financing of world trade by dollar bills has increased greatly since the war for this reason, and is likely to continue to do so in the future.[2] At the present time, both the sterling and the dollar bill are used as international currency.

Referring now to what was said earlier in this chapter regarding finance bills, it will be evident that foreign as well as English merchants can and do avail themselves of the facilities offered by the London accepting houses; and that where a foreign merchant has drawn against a Revolving Credit he will have, before the maturity of the bill, to buy sterling and remit it to the acceptors. He will also have to pay the acceptance commission in sterling. The acceptance business, therefore, as well as ordinary trading operations, will bring bills on London into existence and create corresponding and slightly larger demands for sterling.

To sum up the conclusions of the latter part of this chapter:

(1) Ordinary trade bills come into existence as the result of the export and import of goods.

(2) Bills on London, and corresponding demands for sterling, come into existence as the result of shipments of goods from one part of the world direct to another, without coming to London.

(3) Other things being equal, a surplus of exports over imports will raise the value of a country's currency, and a surplus of imports over exports will lower it.

(4) To avoid misconception, it should be added that

[1] December, 1922.

[2] See Chapter XIV for a brief comparison of London and New York as financial centres.

there are other factors than imports and exports of goods which will create a demand for and a supply of bills; and that the value, in relation to gold, of the currency of the country on which the bills are drawn is also an important element in their price. These matters will be examined in detail later.

(5) The credit facilities supplied by London bring finance bills on London into existence; and if these are drawn abroad there will be a corresponding and slightly larger demand for sterling from abroad to meet these bills when they fall due and to pay London its commission for the use of these facilities.

(6) The actual rates of exchange charged for drafts in foreign currency are based on the prices at which bills on that foreign country can be bought.

APPENDIX TO CHAPTER IV

Specimen Letter of Lien

30th June, 1922.

Messrs. X. & Y., Ltd.,
London, E.C.2.

Dear Sirs,

In consideration of your accepting our draft value £2,500 maturing 30th September/3rd October, 1922, we give you herewith a lien on the goods as per list and copy invoices attached; and we undertake to reimburse you before the due date out of the proceeds of the sales of the said goods and to hold such proceeds as and when received in trust for you.

In payment of your accepting commission, we beg to hand you our cheque value £15 12s. 6d., receipt of which please acknowledge.

Yours faithfully,

CHAPTER V

EXCHANGE TRADING

Methods of quoting rates—Example of fallacies in exchange calculations—Relations between client, provincial bank, head office, foreign exchange broker—Nostro accounts—The foreign exchange trader—Covering transactions—Classes of draft quoted—Tel Quel rates—Forward operations and quotations—Arbitrage operations illustrated.

THE examination of the way foreign currency balances are built up showed that rates of exchange depend on the price of bills. Before proceeding to analyse the factors which determine the price of bills, it seems best to correlate the theory of the last chapter with the practice of exchange trading as handled in the foreign departments of the banks and reported in the daily newspapers.

In the money columns in the daily papers there are, under the heading " Foreign Exchanges " a list of figures preceded by a certain amount of descriptive wording, recording the movements in rates which occurred during the previous day, such as " marks depreciated," " dollars appreciated," etc., etc. The figures formerly represented the foreign exchange rates which were current at the close of business on the previous day in the various foreign centres. They were not the rates quoted in London, but were cabled from the foreign centres opposite the various names. To-day they represent the rates obtaining in London at the close of the previous day's business. These figures are in one or two forms. Either they mean so much of a foreign currency unit to the pound, as in the case of France, Germany, or U.S.A.—3·90 opposite U.S.A. means that you can get 3·90 dollars for £1—or they are in the form of so many pence, or shillings and pence, per foreign unit, as in the case of Brazil, where the figure 8 means that you can get a milreis for 8d.; or in the case of Japan, where the figure of 2s. 4d. means that you can get a yen for that amount. All the rates are quoted in one or other of these two forms.

The difficulty in reading exchange rates is that the prices of currencies are not quoted in the same way as other prices. The rarsing fo the figure which indicates the price of any article is favourable from the seller's point of view, as, for example, is the case in the stock market, of which one is most likely to think when considering exchange matters. A rise in the price of shares is obviously favourable to the holders; but a rise in the rate quoted for sterling may or may not be favourable to the holder. In the case of the dollar, clearly a higher figure does mean a more favourable rate, as it is better for us to get four dollars for our pound than 3·9 dollars. In the case of Brazil the opposite is true: in selling sterling for milreis, it is more advantageous to the seller of sterling to obtain one milreis for every 8d. than for every 10d. In this case the raising of the rate is unfavourable. The rule is that where the exchange is quoted in terms of foreign currency to the pound the high rate is favourable to sterling; where it is quoted in terms of pence per foreign unit, a low rate is favourable to sterling. We have been using the terms "favourable" and "unfavourable" in the sense in which the newspapers frequently use them, i.e. from the point of view of the holder of sterling, i.e. of the potential buyer of foreign currency. It is necessary to bear in mind that when the newspapers say "the French rate went further in our favour," they are speaking from the point of view of the holder of sterling who wishes to buy francs. To the holder of the currency whose rate is in question, e.g. to the English holder of German marks, the significance of the terms "favourable" and "unfavourable" will be exactly the opposite. The lower the rate, i.e. the less marks he has to give up to secure one pound, the better he will be pleased.

Now, looking at the matter from the foreigners' point of view, it will be evident that where the quotation is in terms of foreign currency to the pound, as in the case of francs, marks, and dollars, a rise in the rate means a decline in the value of those currencies, because more francs have to be surrendered to secure a pound. Similarly, a fall in the rate for francs means a rise in their value. It is this point of view which the newspaper writer is taking when, on the rate for francs declining from 52·5 to 52·0 to the pound, he says, "francs appreciated slightly": it is the value which has appreciated.

There is one caution it is necessary to bear in mind. In the news columns of the papers—not in the money columns—one frequently sees the phrase "Yesterday the £1 was worth 18s. in New York, 41s. 6d. in Paris," and so on. That is the wrong way to think about the exchanges. A pound cannot be worth 18s. 6d. in New York, for the simple reason that in New York they do not deal in pounds, shillings, and pence. It can only be worth a certain amount of dollars. If on the day we read that the pound was worth 18s. 6d. in New York we had turned to the back page and read the money column, we should have seen that the pound was worth 4·38 dollars. What was meant was of course that a pound to-day would produce the amount of dollars, which, had the pound been at par value, could have been purchased for 18s. 6d. In other words, at pre-war values the amount of dollars which to-day will purchase £1 would only have purchased 18s. 6d. The statement that the pound was worth 18s. 6d. is a half-truth stated in a form which is sheer nonsense.

This is more than a question of words. Of the errors into which this way of thinking about the exchanges can lead, a good example is the following incident. It is given in full as it is a good exercise in exchange thinking. The subjoined letter appeared in the "Manchester Guardian" of February 27, 1920:—

"I purchased an article some months ago for £600 calculated on $4·75 to the pound sterling, and agreed to pay the difference in the exchange when the goods were delivered. When I paid the cheque the pound was worth $3·25, and the papers of that day boomed the fact that the pound had touched 13s. 3d. One would think, therefore, that I should have to pay 600 times 6s. 9d., equal to £207 10s. But I am told that the difference is £277 10s. or 9s. 3d. for each pound sterling that I have already paid. If that is correct, the pound on the rate of exchange was worth only 10s. 9d. It may be simple to some people, but can anyone make it clear to me?"

Inquiry among the author's classes in Manchester found very few who were able to point out all the fallacies in the above letter. Apart from a small mistake in arithmetic and the ignoring of the fact that his remittance was made at a rate fractionally different from the 3·25 quoted, the writer of the letter may be interested to learn, if he buys this book, that there were three fallacies in his argument.

The first and most fundamental was that the pound was never worth so many shillings and pence in the United States, but so many dollars and cents. His liability was reckoned, and could only be reckoned, in dollars and cents. This is true whether the price was quoted to him in pounds or dollars. If the price was quoted in dollars, the following calculation obtains:—

Price in dollars (600 × 4·75) - - -	= \$2850
His £600 realized dollars (600 × 3·25) -	= \$1950
Difference which he had to pay - -	\$900

These 900 had to be purchased at 3·25, so that the sterling he had to expend was £(900 ÷ 3·25) = 276·923, or £276 18s. 6d.

If, on the other hand, the price was quoted to him in sterling, he had to make up the difference in exchange of \$(4·75 − 3·25) = \$1·5 on every pound, so that he would have to find 600 times \$1·5 = \$900, and to purchase that 900 dollars at 3·25. This entails an expenditure of £276 18s. 6d. as per the previous calculation. The difference between the £276 18s. 6d. at which we arrive and the £277 10s. which he actually had to pay will evidently be accounted for by the fact that at the hour when he paid his cheque, the rate was slightly below 3·25; 3·25 quoted by the newspapers was the closing rate for the day.

Secondly, his reasoning is wrong even if we take his own erroneous standpoint and use his own misleading terms. First of all there is an arithmetical mistake. When the pound was equivalent to \$3·25, it was "worth," in terms of pre-war pounds, $\frac{3 \cdot 25}{4 \cdot 87}$ of 20s. = 13s. 4d., so that the difference to be made up, according to his premises, would not be 6s. 9d. but 6s. 8d. multiplied by 600. But, apart from this arithmetical mistake, his reasoning is wrong even if we start from his own premises. For on the day of purchase the pound was not "worth" 20s.; it was "worth" only $\frac{4 \cdot 75}{4 \cdot 87}$ of 20s. = 19s. 6d.

The amount to be made up would therefore be not 20s. − 13s. 4d., but 19s. 6d. − 13s. 4d. = 6s. 2d.; so that on his own line of reasoning he should have paid not 600 × 6s. 8d. but 600 × 6s. 2d.

Thirdly, in calculating his liability in shillings and

pence, he is throughout calculating in pre-war shillings and pence, whereas the only shillings and pence available to him in which to settle his liability were depreciated coins : the shillings and pence not of pre-war days, nor even of the day of purchase of the goods, but of the day of payment. Paying, as he has to do, in depreciated shillings and pence, he has to pay not only 6s. 2d. per pound, but something additional to make the six-and-twopences which he pays equivalent to the pre-war six-and-twopences in terms of which he has been reckoning.

Had the writer of the letter kept his mind clear of the second and third fallacies, he could, working by his own roundabout methods, have reached the correct result which is properly obtained by our first calculation above. What it was essential to remember, and what he forgot, was that when he thought " the pound is worth so many shillings and pence," what he really meant was " to-day's pound is worth so many pre-war shillings and pence" ; and he should have added, " I have got to provide the equivalent in to-day's shillings of so many pre-war shillings." His calculation would have been as follows :

Number of pounds on which deficiency has to be made up - - - - -	600
Deficiency per pound on day of payment as compared with day of purchase - -	6s. 2d.
Each 6s. 2d. of to-day must, in order to be made equal to the pre-war 6s. 2d., be increased in the ratio of - - - -	$\frac{4{\cdot}867}{3{\cdot}25}$

The liability is therefore

$$6s.\ 2d. \times 600 \times \frac{4{\cdot}867}{3{\cdot}25} \text{ shillings,}$$

or $\frac{£{\cdot}3082 \times 600 \times 4{\cdot}867}{3{\cdot}25} = £276{\cdot}924 = £276\ 18s.\ 6d.$

All his trouble would have been avoided had he remembered that in the United States his pounds were worth so many dollars and cents. Had he remembered that, he would not have presented us with a very interesting example of the wrong way to think about exchange matters.

If we are going to think clearly on the subject of the exchanges, we must avoid half-truths such as that indicated by the statement criticized. We must think of the pound as being worth so much of the currency of the country in question.

The next point in regard to the quotations in the daily papers is that they are double-barrelled—there are two quotations. These two quotations represent buyers and sellers. Suppose, for example, that on any given day the quotation opposite New York is 3·96–3·97 That means if you are buying dollars you will get 3·96 dollars for every pound you expend; if, on the other hand, you have dollars to sell, you will get £1 for every 3·97. If you went to the foreign exchange department of a bank at the time these quotations obtained, they would tell you that dollars were 3·96 buyers and 3·97 sellers, or they might have said 3·96½ middle rate. The difference between the two represents the margin for dealing. That does not mean the margin on which a private individual could encroach if he went into your bank to sell or buy dollars—he could not sell better than 3·97 or buy better than 3·96. It means the margin between the banks themselves and the foreign exchange dealers in London. We will look into the matter more closely, and consider the position of four people in this matter. The four people are: the foreign department of a London bank; the foreign department of its Manchester branch; the outside individual in Manchester, "A," who wants to buy or sell a dollar draft; and the foreign exchange broker in London. Assume that the foreign department in London is quoting to ordinary buyers 3·96, and to ordinary sellers 3·97. It will improve on these rates to its Manchester branch, and will probably quote them 3·96¼ and 3·96¾. Thus the Manchester branch will be able to buy at better rates from its London house than "A" could if he went to London direct. Head office is able to make a better rate for Manchester because London itself, being right in the heart of the foreign exchange market, is able to buy from the foreign exchange broker at a still better rate. They will be doing business with the foreign exchange broker which will be something like 3·96⅜ and 3·96⅝. So far as London is concerned the rates are moving inwards. As a matter of fact, some brokers in London buy from a London head office and sell to them at the same rate, simply working on commission and specializing in certain currencies, just as some merchants and manufacturers' agents work entirely on a commission basis. Thus the Manchester branch has the margins between 96 and 96¼ (buying) and between 96¾ and 97 (selling); the London head office has the margins between 96¼ and 96⅜ and between 96¾ and 96⅝; the broker, if he is not working on commission, has the margin between 96⅜ and 96⅝. This example is taken from the dollar exchange, which is one of the steadiest, and where the margins are consequently small and the risks few or none. In the case of the exchanges with wider fluctuations the margins are very much greater.

The broker, after a sale of currency to the bank, sends to the purchasing bank a contract note stating particulars of the currency sold and the name of the seller; this enables the bank to instruct the seller where to pay the currency. The currency is not in the form of foreign notes, but of a draft on a foreign bank; and it is paid, not to the bank itself but by its instructions to its foreign currency account in the foreign town in question. Banks keep such accounts in the principal centres abroad. They are known as " Nostro " accounts (*Latin* = our). It is on these accounts that the foreign drafts issued by banks to their customers who have bought foreign currency are issued, and from them that mail and telegraphic transfers[1] are made. Proceeds of bills and coupons sent for collection similarly go to swell the Nostro account. In the case of sale of currency by the bank to the broker, a similar contract note is passed by the broker to his purchasers, from whom the selling bank receives instructions where to pay the currency. Payment is made, of course, out of a Nostro account.

The actual work of buying and selling currencies in a bank is performed by the exchange trader, who is usually " second-man " in the foreign department, i.e. second-in-command to the manager of the foreign department. The most go-ahead of the provincial branches of the joint-stock banks have now direct telephonic communication with their London head office, by means of which they are advised of the fluctuations in rates from minute to minute. The exchange trader's aim all the time is to balance his sales and his purchases, so that he is left neither with foreign currency on his hands nor with a liability in respect of currency which he has sold but not yet bought in. His aim, in other words, is not to make big profits by gambling on the prospects of rises or falls in exchange rates, but to accumulate margins and take as little risk as possible. He will, therefore, in so far as his sales are not covered by his purchases, cover by buying immediately from his own head office, and in so far as his purchases are not disposed of by his sales, sell immediately to his own head office. The head office trader in turn will sell to the exchange dealers; and it is the higgling of the market between head office

[1] See p. 6.

traders and exchange dealers, who in turn have connexions abroad, which ultimately makes the final rates.

The next point to refer to in regard to the rates quoted in the daily papers is the class of draft quoted for. Different centres quote for different classes of draft. The principal kinds of drafts quoted for are:

Cable transfers.	8-day drafts.
Sight drafts.	90-day drafts.

A cable transfer is the means used by a man in New York who wants to pay a man in London at once. He goes into the offices of a New York bank, instructs them to cable a certain amount of money to someone in London, and pays them a certain quantity of dollars. The bank immediately cables its London correspondents, and the latter firm pay immediately they receive the cable. That is the meaning of a cable transfer. The cable rate is the rate at which the dollars paid by the man in New York are exchanged for the sterling which the payee in London receives.

A sight draft is a draft payable at sight and goes by mail. "A" has to pay a creditor in Paris. "A" sends him a draft in francs on some French bank, payable at sight. The sight rate is the rate at which "A" buys that draft in francs from a London bank: it represents the rate at which sterling is converted into francs payable at sight in Paris.

Eight and ninety-day drafts mean drafts payable 11 (8 plus 3 days of grace) and 93 days respectively after sight. The classes of drafts quoted in the newspapers for each of the principal centres are:

Paris - - - - -	Sight drafts.
Brussels - - - -	,, ,,
Berlin - - - - -	,, ,,
Other European centres -	,, ,,

New York - - -	Cable, sight, 60-day.
Oriental Exchanges	Telegraphic transfers.
Egypt - - - - - -	Sight rate.
Brazil - - - - - -	90 days.
Argentine - - - - -	90 ,,

The sight rate is known as "Short Exchange," and the three months' rate as "Long Exchange." The three months' rate can be calculated from the short rate, and vice versa[1] The point to remember in making these calculations is that when we buy a sight draft we are paying a dealer pounds down for francs at sight; for practical purposes we are paying pounds now and getting in exchange francs now. When, on the other hand, we buy a three months' draft, we are paying pounds now, and getting francs which will not materialize until three months hence. It will be evident that, in consideration of waiting, we must in the second case receive more francs for the same number of pounds than in the first: the long rate, in other words, will be higher in this case than the short rate. If we are dealing not with the currency which is quoted in terms of foreign units to the pound, but with one which is quoted in terms of so many pence to the foreign unit, with the milreis, for example, the long rate will be lower than the short: for the buyer has to be benefited in consideration of waiting, and the only way to benefit him is to reduce the number of pence he pays for each milreis.

Particular rates can be made for bills which have periods of between one and three months to run, e.g. 73 days. Such rates are known as Tel Quel (= such as it is) rates. They can be calculated from either the sight rate or the three months' rate on the principle indicated in the foregoing paragraph. They will be

[1] For details of the calculations involved, see Spalding: "Foreign Exchange and Foreign Bills," p. 48.

more favourable to the buyer of the bill than the sight rate (i.e. more francs to the pound or fewer pence to the milreis), for the buyer has to wait for his claim to the foreign currency to mature; less favourable to him than the three months' rate, for he has not to wait so long.

With one exception, bills for periods longer than three months are not common in exchange markets. A merchant who desires to discount a longer-dated bill with his bank invites reflections as to the financial soundness of the customers with whom he is doing business: why do they require such long credit? Bills of longer than three months' maturity are drawn, but generally their use is to be held as security for a debt rather than to serve as currency. The exception occurs in the South American trade, where bills at 120 days are customary and recognized.

An operation which demands a word of explanation is that of buying and selling exchange forward. Merchants do not as a rule wish to gamble in exchange, and a merchant doing business to-day with one of the numerous countries whose currency is subject to frequent fluctuations generally avoids risk by the above-named operation. If he is due to receive or to have to pay a certain quantity of foreign currency at a future date, or within a given period, he sells this currency or buys, as the case may be, in advance. If he is an exporter due to receive payment in currency, he agrees to deliver to the bank on a certain day, or within a certain period, that quantity of that currency. Conversely if he is an importer due to pay a certain quantity of currency, he agrees to buy that quantity on a certain day or within a certain period. The transaction in each case is made at a rate fixed at the time. The merchant limits his liability to a definite quantity of sterling; the bank has means not available to the merchant lessening the liability of which it has relieved him. Where the bank is the forward seller, and the amount is small, it may purchase spot currency and hold it until such time as the customer requires it. Where the amount is larger, the bank in turn may buy forward. In any case, it can, if it desires, rely on its balances abroad for delivery. A forward sale, again, may be set off against a long-dated bill on the foreign centre in question, maturing on or a little before the date of delivery of the currency. Or such a long-dated bill maturing later than the said date might be discounted on or before the date of delivery. Similarly when currency is bought forward from a client, the purchase can be covered by a forward sale. Or, if, e.g. delivery of the currency is to be made by the seller to the bank in two months' time, the bank can now sell two months' drafts on the foreign centre in question.

The rates for forward purchases and sales of course vary from those for spot transactions. They may be more or less favourable to the buyer, according to the opinion held by the foreign exchange market of the likelihood that during the near future the currency in question will appreciate or depreciate. Thus, e.g. on July 20, 1922, the " Manchester Guardian " quoted the rates on certain centres for settlement one month forward as follows. The rates for two and three months forward are usually approximately twice or thrice those quoted for one month forward.

New York - -	$\frac{3}{16}$ to $\frac{5}{16}$ cent over spot.
Brussels - -	4 to 3 centimes under spot.
Paris - - -	5 to 7 centimes over spot.
Berlin - -	10 to 15 marks over spot (nominal).
Italy - -	1 centesimo under to one over spot.

The last operation which requires mention is that of arbitrage. Exchange arbitrage is similar to the corresponding operation in stock and shares. The arbitrage dealer, or cambist, is an exchange dealer in country "A" who buys or sells currency of country "B" in the foreign exchange market of country "C" in order immediately to sell it again at a profit in country "A" or "B." Suppose, for example, that Berlin has been making heavy payments for American wheat, and the New York Exchange has moved against Berlin to the extent that in Berlin the dollar is quoted at 510 marks. The Berlin-London rate is at the minute 2,200 marks to the pound; the London-New York rate is £1 = 4·4 dollars. A Berlin merchant expending 2,200 marks in purchasing dollars will secure \$(2,200 ÷ 510) = \$4·03. But a Berlin exchange dealer buying sterling will for 2,200 marks secure £1, with which in London he can buy \$4·44. That \$4·4 he can immediately sell to the merchant in Berlin for 4·4 × 510 marks = 2,244 marks, thus making 44 marks profit. The Berlin dealer will carry out some such transaction as the following. He will wire his London correspondent to buy thirty thousand dollars at a price up to 500 marks per dollar. From the London correspondent's point of view the deal is acceptable, for it outlines itself thus in his mind:

Selling \$30,000 to Berlin at Mk. 500 per dollar

produces in sterling, $\frac{30{,}000 \times 500}{2{,}200} = £6{,}818{\cdot}182$

Cost of buying \$30,000 at 4·44 is $\frac{30{,}000}{4{\cdot}44} = £6{,}756{\cdot}756$

Balance, being profit - - - £61·426

The London correspondent buys the dollars by

telephone and wires the Berlin dealer, who immediately sells them. His calculations are as follows:

Selling $30,000 at 510 produces -	Mk. 15,300,000
Buying $30,000 at 500 costs - - -	Mk. 15,000,000
Balance, being profit - -	Mk. 300,000

The transactions might be very much more complicated than this—a whole literature has grown up on this section of the subject alone; but the above example illustrates—clearly, it is hoped—the principles of arbitrage.[1] Speed is the essence of the operation: simultaneously with the transaction of buying dollars in London, the Berlin dealer must sell the equivalent quantity of dollars in Berlin. He dare not allow time to elapse because the rates are likely to fluctuate. Apart from any other causes making for fluctuations, other dealers will be doing the same as he. Exchange arbitrage thus consists of utilizing for profit the different conditions temporarily obtained in other markets, and is a levelling operation which is always tending to make conditions in the various markets uniform.

In the case of a financial house which has branches in two centres, an arbitrage operation such as the above is easier to carry through, for in such a case the operation has to provide a profit margin for one party only. In the above example, if the London correspondent had been the agent or the branch of the Berlin operator, the former could have carried through the transaction even if the dollar rate had meantime fallen lower than 4·44. He could have carried it through at any rate down to 4·40 (2,200 ÷ 500), for down to this rate he could have

[1] The actual profit margins which obtain are usually much smaller than those assumed in the above example.

bought the dollars and remitted them to Berlin at the stipulated price of Mk. 500 per dollar without suffering any loss, thus :

Paid : Cost of \$30,000 at 4·40

$$= \frac{30{,}000}{4{\cdot}40} = £6{,}818{\cdot}182$$

Received : Value of \$30000 at Mk. 500

= Mk. 15,000,000, worth at 2,200

$$= £\frac{15{,}000{,}000}{2{,}200} = £6{,}818{\cdot}182$$

Meantime, the principal's margin in Berlin between 500 and 510 would have remained intact.

An operation similar in principle can be carried through in shares or bonds which have a market in more than one country. When exchange rates are stable, the price of, say, Royal Dutch shares in Amsterdam will be a sum in florins, which, when converted into sterling at the current rate of exchange, will be equivalent to the price quoted on the London Stock Exchange. When exchange rates move, the price of these shares will move with them, tending always to the establishment of a common price level in the centres on which they are quoted; but on occasion the adjustment of share prices may lag a little behind the movement of exchange rates. Thus, following a rise in the London-Amsterdam rate, which means a decline in the value of florins, it may happen that Royal Dutch shares are cheaper in Amsterdam than in London, i.e. they can be bought in Amsterdam for a sum in florins, which, when converted into sterling at the now current rate, is fractionally less than the price quoted in London. In these circumstances, a dealer in either centre, or in another centre such as Paris, may be able to snatch a profit by telegraphing a buying order for so many shares to Amsterdam and, as soon as he receives the reply wire advising that the purchase has been made, selling them in London. This operation would itself tend to raise the price in Amsterdam and to depress it in London, and so to establish a new price level common to both centres.

CHAPTER VI

DOCUMENTARY BILLS AND CREDITS

Clean and documentary bills—Letter of hypothecation—D/A and D/P drafts—Bankers' advances against bills—Negotiation before acceptance—Documentary credits—Confirmed and unconfirmed credits—Bills for collection—Payable and interest clauses—Acceptance supra protest.

IT has been explained in outline how foreign bills feed the foreign currency balances of the banks, and how the exchange trader operates on those balances at rates which are fixed by the factors ruling in the foreign exchange market. Before we proceed to analyse these factors,[1] it is best to complete our mental picture of the foreign exchange world by examining in detail some of the more important credit operations between bankers and merchants centreing round the foreign bill. This chapter is accordingly devoted to the detailed procedure for dealing with foreign bills.

The first distinction to make is that between clean and documentary bills. A documentary bill is a bill which has attached to it the shipping documents covering the goods in respect of which the bill is drawn. A clean bill is a bill without such documents attached. The documents in question are:

(*a*) Invoice.
(*b*) Bill of lading.
(*c*) Consular invoice.
(*d*) Insurance policy or insurance certificate.
(*e*) Letter of hypothecation, particular or general.

Invoice, bill of lading, and consular invoice are straight-

[1] See Chapter VII.

forward enough, but we must say a word about the letter of hypothecation and the insurance policy. A letter or certificate of hypothecation is an instrument in and by virtue of which the drawer of the draft makes legal acknowledgments which constitute any holder of the draft also the holder of the bill of lading and insurance certificate as collateral security. What that means is this: the bank has the draft, it has the documents covering the goods, and it requires a further document to show that it has a legal right to the document covering the goods. A hypothecation certificate is that document. It gives a banker a good title to the documents which cover the goods. A hypothecation certificate may be particular or general. Where the transaction is an isolated one, the bank will have a form of letter of hypothecation applicable to that kind of draft, probably a printed form which the drawer of the draft will sign and send along with the bill and documents. Where, however, the business is a regular, steady, and sound one, conducted by exporters well known to the bank, and the foreign importers also well known to the bank, then it is quite likely that the bank will be satisfied with a general letter of hypothecation, by which the drawer of the draft hypothecates to the bank all the documents attached to all his drafts which the bank discounts for him. In such a case, again, the bank will not require an insurance policy itself, but will accept in lieu thereof an insurance certificate, i.e. a certificate from a firm of insurance brokers to the effect that the goods in question have been insured.

The next point in connexion with documentary drafts is the distinction between D/A and D/P drafts. A D/A draft means that the documents attached to the draft are to be surrendered on acceptance of the draft; a D/P draft means that the documents are not to be surrendered until the draft is paid. The custom is for the drawers of the bill, when sending it to their bank for negotiation, or for collection and remittance of the proceeds as the case may be, to cover it with a letter in which they say that the documents attached to the draft are to be surrendered only on acceptance, or only on payment of the draft. Or, alternatively, in place of such a letter, they attach a slip to the draft embodying the same statement. Where nothing is stated it is always understood that a documentary draft is a D/P draft. From the point of view of the bank making the advances against the documentary draft, clearly the D/P bill is the safer. It is conceivable that the drawees might accept a D/A draft, get the documents, and then dishonour the bill. In the case of a D/P draft, they cannot get the documents until they have paid the bill. However, as we shall see, both kinds of drafts are suitable on occasion for the bank to advance money against, while on occasion neither may be suitable. It all depends upon the circumstances of each particular case. There are some markets, South American chiefly, where business is nearly always done with D/A drafts, and in other markets it frequently happens that where the drawers are starting business with the drawees they will use D/P drafts for the first two or three shipments, and D/A drafts afterwards.

We now come to the question of banks' advances against drafts. A documentary draft may be negotiated either before or after acceptance. Here we need only repeat in outline the case taken earlier on, when we saw how foreign bills served as currency.[1] We took the case where a British firm was shipping goods to Sweden and drawing on the Swedish consignees, whom we called Franssons. The drawers would draw, let us say, a sixty days' sight draft D/A on Franssons ; and the draft might be dealt with in one of various ways.

[1] See Chapter IV.

(*a*) If the drawers have an agent in Stockholm, they would send the documentary draft to that agent, the agent would present the draft to Franssons, get it accepted by them, and hand over to Franssons the documents. Franssons could then get the goods while the agent might return the draft to the British exporter, who would then sell it either to his bank or to a London bill-broker, from either of whom the draft would find its way on to the London foreign exchange market.

(*b*) If the British exporter had no agent in Stockholm, but nevertheless did a good business in Sweden, which necessitated paying out as well as paying in in Sweden, he might very well keep a foreign currency account at a bank in Sweden, let us say the Skandinaviska Kreditaktiebolaget in Stockholm. In that case, he would send the draft to that bank, they would present it to Franssons, get it accepted and hand over the documents; and having now the draft in the form of a clean bill, the bank might either hold it until the draft matured, then present it for payment and credit the British exporter's account at that date, or it might discount the bill at once and credit the British exporter's account at once.

(*c*) Again, in place of the agent returning the draft to the British exporter, he himself might have sold it to his Swedish bank, say the Nordiska Handelsbanken, in Stockholm. In return he would receive this bank's draft in kroner, drawn on another Stockholm bank, which he would send to the British exporter to be sold on the London Foreign Exchange market.

These are the outlines of the various procedures which might be followed. They all have this in common: that the draft is not discounted until it has been accepted. In that sense the foreign bill on Franssons is just like an ordinary home trade bill of exchange.

Now suppose that instead of being a D/A draft it had been a D/P draft. In that case Franssons would not have been able to get the goods until they had not only accepted, but also paid the draft. It may be asked, What good was the draft to them ? They would be able to inspect the goods, and during the 60 days sell them, so that immediately they got the documents they could hand them straight over to the ultimate buyers. There is another possibility in regard to a D/P draft : Franssons might like to pay under a rebate ; in other words, they might not wait until the 60 days were up, but pay the draft before, and obtain a rebate of the proportionate amount of interest. It is of course possible that after Franssons had originally accepted the D/P draft and given it back to the bank, the bank might have detached the draft from the documents, and sold it clean. In that case Franssons could still have paid the draft under rebate of a proportionate amount of the interest, and the bank would have given them the documents, together with a guarantee that when the holder of the draft presented it for payment the bank itself would pay. Even a D/P draft can in that way become a clean bill.

All these cases are relatively simple. They all have the characteristic that there is no question of discounting until the draft is accepted. Now we come to a more complicated case, in which the money is advanced against the draft before it is accepted. It is quite evident that there must be some kind of arrangement whereby that can be done, because the procedure we have outlined, while useful for Sweden and the nearer continental countries, would not be of very much use in regard to Eastern and South American markets, and we find accordingly that there are ways whereby the banks can and do advance money against drafts before acceptance. To such an extent in fact is that the case, that there are markets and trades in which it is customary for the bank to advance money not only against D/P bills before acceptance, but also against D/A drafts before acceptance, and sometimes even without the original documents accompanying the drafts. It is customary, for instance, in certain lines of business in Brazil for the original bill of lading to be sent direct to the Brazilian importer by the British exporter, and the documentary draft has attached to it, in place of the original bill of lading, only a duplicate. That means that the importer in Brazil can get possession of the goods without even accepting the draft. Nevertheless, it is customary for one of the first-class foreign banks in London to advance to British exporters of the first class the face value of such D/A drafts. The whole fact of the matter is this: in dealing with the question of banks' advances against documentary drafts, it is simply a question of deciding each case on its own merits. Inquiries have to be made regarding the customs of the particular trade in question, the class of business being done, and the financial standing and repute of the drawer and the drawee. When a bank has made an advance against a documentary draft before acceptance, the procedure is for it to advise the drawer when the draft has been accepted, and again when it has been paid, at the same time sending him a statement relating to the bill. The statement will run in some such form as this:

"We beg to advise you that your remittance No. 4672/5183 [firm's number of draft and bank's own number] has been paid. As we advanced you the face value of this draft, we shall be obliged if you will refund us the amount undernoted.

	£	s.	d.
Commission, @ ⅛ per cent. - -		6	4
Foreign Bill Stamps - - -		5	4
Postage - - - - -		1	0
Cables - - - - - -		2	6
—— Days' Interest, @ —— per cent.	1	19	3
	£2	14	5"

Such a statement is sent where the bank advanced the face value of the draft. Frequently, however, the bank advances a proportion of the face value, say 80 per cent., paying to the drawer the balance, less charges, only when advice of payment is received. The bank's statement to the drawer then reads as follows:

By Proceeds of your Draft No......... -		£118	11	1
Less—Commission, @ —— per cent. - - - - -	s. d. 6 4			
Foreign Bill Stamps -	5 4			
Postage - - - - -	1 0			
			12	8
		117	18	5
To amount advances against above bill - - -	95 0 0			
Interest —— days, @ —— per cent. - - - - -	1 19 3			
		96	19	3
Balance in cheque herewith		£20	19	2

The rates of interest charged on advances against bills vary in accordance with the movement of rates generally in the money market.[1]

The inquiries which a bank will make when asked to advance money against a documentary bill vary with each particular case. If, for example, a bank is approached by, let us say, an English export firm of small proportions and little standing, the bank will probably want to know a good deal about the business

[1] See Chapter X.

to which the draft relates. The firm asking for the advance may be asked to produce the order from the foreign importer and the invoice from the English manufacturer from whom it obtained the goods. The bank will also want to know whether the foreign importer is a firm of good standing, not likely to refuse to take up the goods, and if the English manufacturer is also a firm of good standing, whose goods can be relied upon. If all these conditions are fulfilled, then the bank will probably make an advance of perhaps 80 per cent. of the value. If these conditions are not complied with, they will not.

Another case of a bill being negotiated before acceptance occurs where an accepting house has agreed to accept bills drawn upon itself up to a certain amount. If, for example, a Brazilian exporter of coffee could go to his bank, and produce a letter from one of the big merchant bankers in London, agreeing to accept bills drawn on themselves at so many days date, up to a certain amount, accompanied by shipping documents covering a certain shipment, in that case the bank at Rio de Janeiro would have no hesitation in making an advance to the face value of the bill, simply because it knows the status of the London accepting house.

The next subject to be dealt with in connexion with documentary drafts is that of documentary credits. Documentary credits serve as a means of financing foreign business in cases where otherwise the possibility of negotiating drafts before acceptance would not exist. In the case of a documentary credit, there are four parties to take into consideration: the buyer, the buyer's bank, the seller, and a bank in the seller's country. Assume the buyer to be a London merchant, the seller a New York exporter. The buyer's London bank is "A" and the seller's bank in New York is "B." The terms of sale of the goods require the opening of a credit with

" B " available against shipping documents. The procedure in very broad outline is this: the buyer instructs " A " to open a credit with " B " in favour of the sellers to cover the shipment of the goods in question. " A " communicates with " B " by mail or telegram, and " B " notifies the sellers that a credit has been opened with " B " to finance the shipment of the goods specified in the advice. The principle is that " A," having charge of the buyer's account and being therefore in a position to debit that account, is able without risk to itself to authorize " B " to make payments; " B " is willing to act on the authorization of another bank; while the seller is willing to ship on learning from " B," his own bank, that " B " will make payment against the shipping documents. The actual manner in which " B " will make payment varies according to the terms of the credit as transmitted by " A " from the buyer. (1) " B " may pay cash over the counter in exchange for the shipping documents either unaccompanied by any draft, or (2) accompanied by a sight draft on " B," or (3) " B " may, in exchange for the shipping documents, accept, say, a 90 days' sight draft drawn by the seller on " B." Or again (4) " B " may negotiate a sight or date draft on the buyer. Such a draft will be in dollars, for a seller who is in a strong enough position to demand the opening of a credit before he ships the goods will certainly insist on the terms of that credit enabling him to draw in his own currency.

In all four cases " B " will debit " A's " account in its books with the amount expended as on the date of payment; or alternatively if " A " does not keep an account with " B," the latter will obtain a refund of its payments from the local bank which keeps " A's " dollar balance in New York. " B," or the New York bank which keeps " A's " account, will advise " A " by cable of the dollar amount with which " A " has been debited, and will confirm by mail.

In case (4), where the procedure has been by way of "B" negotiating a dollar draft on the buyer, "B" will mail the draft to "A" and "A" will present it to the drawee, i.e. the buyer, for payment. It will be paid by "A" debiting the buyer's account in its books with the amount of sterling required, on the day of payment, to buy a sight draft on New York for the amount of dollars specified on the draft. The draft itself will contain a clause providing that the drawee shall also pay interest for the period from the date of the draft to the date of payment at the stated rate. The debiting of the buyer's account in "A's" books with this interest amount will compensate "A" for the loss of interest in New York on the amount with which "A" was debited by "B."

In the other three cases, (1), (2), and (3), "A" will then debit the buyer's account in its books, as on the date on which payment was made in New York, with the sterling equivalent of the dollars with which it has been debited in New York. The question arises as to the rate of exchange applied. Theoretically, the rate should be that at which "A" has presumably had to replenish its dollar balance, i.e. the cable rate obtaining on the day when it received cable advice that the payment had been made. When we speak of the cable rate we mean, of course, the cable rate quoted in the London exchange market adjusted by the bank's exchange trader in the manner already described.[1] But in actual fact "A" will have the option of two rates: first the one mentioned, and second the earlier rate obtaining on the day when the buyer gave instructions for the credit to be opened. "A" will almost certainly choose the rate less favourable to sterling, i.e. the rate at which the given quantity of dollars paid out by "B" means a greater amount of sterling; and will debit the buyer with the greater

[1] See Chapter V.

amount, irrespective of the rate at which it has in fact replenished its New York balance. The margin between the rates which it has applied to the buyer and that at which it actually covered its sale of dollars to him represents a profit on exchange to the bank over and above the normal margin on the rates charged to its customers.

A point arises in regard to the words "shipping documents" specified in the advice opening the credit. The documents required are of course the invoice, bill of lading, consular invoice, hypothecation certificate, and insurance policy. But the question may be important as to whether a policy is actually required or whether an insurance certificate, which in commercial usage is more or less equivalent to an insurance policy, will do? In practice some banks will accept what is commonly known as an insurance certificate in place of an insurance policy. An insurance certificate is really an insurance broker's contract note to produce the policy. Another form of insurance certificate consists of a certificate from the shippers of the goods to the effect that the goods have been insured under a floating policy. Still another form of insurance certificate is common in the United States, consisting of a certificate signed by the holder of the floating policy and countersigned by the insurance company which issued the floating policy. Now the isssue is, will any one of those documents serve in place of an insurance policy, given that the terms on which the bank is authorized to negotiate the bills require that the bills be accompanied by shipping documents including insurance policy? The actual procedure followed by banks varies. Some banks insist upon the production of the full insurance policy, and thereby succeed in creating considerable difficulty in the export trade, and in making merchants wait for their money. Other banks will accept an insurance certificate in the first sense, i.e.

a broker's contract note to produce the policy. That, however, makes the bank itself liable in respect of any claim which may be made by the drawee of the draft by reason of the fact that the insurance policy has not accompanied the draft. A ruling to that effect has been laid down in a number of cases,[1] and legally it is quite certain that where an insurance policy is specified, an insurance certificate will not suffice. Nothing will suffice except the policy. However, there is an easy way out of the difficulty created by the conflict of legal rule and commercial practice: any bank will be safe in accepting a certificate where a policy is stipulated for provided that in addition to the certificate it gets also from the importer a letter of indemnity. A letter of indemnity is a letter signed by the exporter, and countersigned by the exporter's own bank, to the effect that the exporter agrees to hold the bank advancing the money indemnified against any claims that may be made against it by reason of the fact that it has accepted the insurance certificate in place of the insurance policy.

A letter of indemnity will also be obtained by a banker who pays out of a credit which stipulates for clean bills of lading, whereas the actual bills of lading are marked "a few bags torn."

A documentary credit such as we are discussing may be either confirmed or unconfirmed. The difference between the two is that in the case of the unconfirmed credit "B" does not guarantee, as principal, that the draft drawn under the terms of the credit will be duly honoured. The implication and the difference are best illustrated by comparing the two forms of letter sent out by a well-known bank advising sellers of the opening of

[1] *Livingstone* v. *Ireland* (1872) is the leading (House of Lords) case, with which *Wilson Holgate* v. *Belgian Grain & Produce Co.* (1919) and *Diamond Alkali Export Corporation, Ltd.* v. *H. Bourgeois* (1922) are in line.

a confirmed and unconfirmed credit respectively. The two letters are in exactly the same form with the exception of the last sentence. In the case of the confirmed credit the last sentence reads :

" We undertake that all drafts drawn in conformity with the terms of this credit will meet with due honour on presentation, provided they are marked as being so drawn."

In the case of the unconfirmed credit the last sentence reads :

" We have no authority from our clients to confirm this credit or to guarantee the acceptance or payment of drafts drawn thereagainst. The credit is therefore subject to cancellation without notice, and the above particulars are for your guidance only."

From the point of view of the seller, therefore, the difference between the two forms of credit amounts practically to this : that the confirmed credit is irrevocable, whereas the unconfirmed can be revoked at any time by instructions. That difference appears clearly from two letters sent out by another bank relating to a confirmed and an unconfirmed credit :

" Confirmed Credit No.——. Kindly note under instructions by telegram we have been requested by ——— [a foreign bank] to open a confirmed credit in your favour on account of ——— [the foreign client] for £—— available by your drafts on us at sight against the following documents :

" Invoice issued in the name of———

" Bills of Lading, full set, issued to order and endorsed in blank.

"Insurance policy, marine and war, covering particular average evidencing shipment of the goods.

"Shipment to be effected on or before —— per S.S. —— from —— to ——. Drafts drawn under this credit must be presented to us on or before 28th February, 1922. All drafts must bear the number and reference mentioned above, and we undertake to honour such drafts on presentation provided they are drawn and presented in conformity with the terms of this credit."

"Unconfirmed Credit No.——. We beg to inform you that a credit has been open with us in your favour by order and for account of —— [the foreign clients] to the extent of £—— available at sight against delivery of the following documents:

"Invoice.

"Bills of Lading, full set relative to shipment of goods. As we have no authority to confirm this credit to you, we are merely passing on this advice on the understanding that it is not intended to convey any engagement on the part of this bank nor any responsibility for the use you may make of this communication, as our clients' instructions may be withdrawn at any time."

It is evident that from the point of view of the merchant the difference between a confirmed and an unconfirmed credit is that the former is irrevocable and the latter can be revoked. From the point of view of the banker the difference is that in the case of the confirmed credit the banker does, and in the case of the unconfirmed credit the banker does not, himself guarantee as principal to the seller that the seller's draft drawn in accordance with that credit will be met.

Unfortunately we are compelled to leave there the question of confirmed and unconfirmed credits. Beyond that point the law is vague. Most parts of the banking law are reasonably clear. Bankers are fortunate in that the banking law has been codified in the Bills of Exchange Act, but this subject of confirmed and unconfirmed credits has not been fully elucidated, and what the rights and liabilities of the various parties to credits are, in the event of one or other of them not fulfilling their obligations, has not yet been settled authoritatively in the courts. It has not yet been made certain what the position of a banker would be who paid out money under an unconfirmed credit which was revoked after he had paid the money out in ignorance of revocation.

On the general subject of credits it may be added that the liability which the banker incurs in opening a credit is identical with the liability he incurs in making advances,[1] and a corresponding amount of care is therefore necessary. Thus in regard to shipping documents it will have been observed in one of the letters quoted that the bills of lading are to be made out to order, and endorsed in blank: this is in order that the banker can if necessary get control of the goods. There is also this further safeguard employed in some cases: where the bank "A" is asked to open a credit for its clients, it inquires of those clients as to whether they themselves have sold the goods; if they have the bank may strengthen its own position by requiring the final purchasers themselves to open a credit through their own bank. That credit will of course be at least equal in amount to, if not greater than, the amount of the credit which bank "A" has itself opened. The second credit is known as a counter-credit, and the operation relating to the opening of these two credits, the second of which balances and safeguards the first, is technically known as "marrying credits."[2]

[1] See article on "The Financing of Foreign Trade" in the "Banker's Magazine" of December, 1919.

[2] For a full description of this procedure, see article cited in foregoing footnote.

By that procedure the banker " A " who is first asked to open a credit has security afforded not only by his own client, but also by the second purchaser and the latter's bank.

Documentary credit business has increased considerably since the war. It affords a means of doing business suitable to the decline in business confidence which has been a natural result of the war. It is likely that this growth in the documentary credit business will continue : first because there are at present no signs, and no reason why there should be signs, of a restoration of business confidence to the extent to which it existed before the war ; and secondly because this documentary credit business corresponds to the natural specialization of functions. Bankers are the specialized dealers of the financial world in credit and finance, and this documentary credit business means in effect the putting of the finance and credit side of business transactions in their hands. In other words, it is the banker's business to know to what extent credit can safely be given.

A few isolated points remain to be considered in connexion with foreign bills. The first is that of bills for Collection. A bill sent for collection may of course be either D/A or D/P, either sight or date. As contrasted with the bill which is negotiated or against which an advance is made, a bill for collection is accepted for collection only, and the drawer's account is credited only when the bill is advised by the collecting bank on the other side as having been paid. This raises the question : How are foreign bills paid ? The question of course relates only to bills drawn in sterling on a foreign centre. Obviously where a bill is drawn by an English firm on a Swedish one in Stockholm in kroner, then clearly it will be paid in kroner. What we have to consider is the case of a bill drawn by an English firm on a Swedish firm in sterling. The Swedish drawee can of course only pay in kroner. The question is at what rate he is to pay kroner for the sterling specified on the bill. The rule is, subject to the bill not being claused in any particular way, and subject to their not being any overriding trade custom, that the rate of exchange for a bill in sterling on a foreign centre is the rate ruling in that centre for sight drafts on London on the day of maturity of the bill. In the case named, the Swedish drawee will have to hand over to the collecting bank in Stockholm such an amount of kroner as will on the date of maturity of the bill, purchase a sight draft on London to the face value of the bill. Supposing for example the bill is for £20, and there is no interest clause in it, and the rate for sight drafts on London on the day of maturity is 18 kr. = £1, then the amount of kroner the drawee will have to pay is $18 \times 20 = 360$ kr. The collecting bank in Stockholm will of course advise the collecting bank in London which sent it the bill for collection that the bill has been paid, and will send them a statement showing so many kroner to their credit, being the quantity of kroner paid by the drawee less collecting charges and commission. The London bank which received the bill from the drawer for collection will on receipt of that statement advise the drawer that the bill has been paid and that his account has been credited with the face value of the bill less collecting charges and commission charged by the home collecting bank. It may be of course that the drawer is in the habit of drawing a number of drafts on Sweden, and that he has payments to make in Sweden; in that case he will very likely find it to his advantage to keep a foreign currency account at a Swedish bank, and in that case he will send his bills for collection not through his own bank here, but direct to his Swedish bank, thus saving himself the commission to the English bank, which he would otherwise have to pay.

To avoid any doubt arising, a "payable" clause is generally inserted in a bill reading, "Payable at the rate for demand drafts on London." Frequently it is a little more precise: "Payable at the drawing rate for the bank's demand drafts on London." An example of such a bill is the following:

"At sixty days' sight pay this first of Exchange (second and third being unpaid) to the order of —— Bank the sum of £—— with interest added hereto at 6 per cent. per annum from date hereof to approximate due date of arrival of remittance in London.

"Payable at the current drawing rate for the —— Bank's draft at sight on London.

"Value received," etc., etc.

That is a slightly more precise clause than that previously employed, and means payable at the rate at which the collecting bank's branch in the place on which the bill is drawn can draw on their London correspondents. The reason for naming the bank is simply that there may be two or three slightly different rates for demand drafts on London according to the quality of the drafts, and for that reason, in order to avoid any possibility of argument on the other side, the name of the bank is inserted. The rate at which the bank named can draw on their London correspondents will vary in accordance with the general fluctuations of exchange rates between the foreign centre in question and London.

If in a foreign centre there is a particular custom governing the payments of drafts in sterling, then the bill will be claused in accordance with that custom. In Brazil, for example, it is the custom to pay, not by sight drafts on London, but by 90 days' sight drafts on London, and bills to Brazil are customarily claused accordingly: "Payable at the current drawing rate for

90 days' sight drafts on London." Similarly in the Argentine, where there are two currencies in existence, the gold peso and the paper peso, bills are frequently claused: "Payable in gold currency at the current drawing rate for sight drafts on London." Where there is a particular custom in the market on which the bill is drawn, it is most desirable that the bill should be claused in accordance with it, otherwise it is extremely likely there will be trouble at the other end. If for example a drawee in Brazil, when he pays sterling drafts on himself, customarily does it by handing over to the bank the number of milreis which will purchase a 90 days' sight draft on London, and on one occasion he is told to hand over the larger number of milreis that are required to purchase a sight draft on London, he will probably refuse. Again, a bill may be claused "Exchange as per Endorsement," which means that the rate of payment is to be the rate endorsed on the bill. Formerly it was the custom for the collecting bank to endorse the rate; latterly, however, differences have occurred between the drawee and the collecting bank at the other end, and in consequence banks sometimes now insist on the seller of the bill himself endorsing the rate, so that in case of dispute the drawee and drawer can settle it between themselves.

Where an advance has been made by a banker against a bill which is paid by means of a 90 days' sight draft, the interest of which the banker claims the refund, or which he deducts from his advance, as the case may be, is charged for the whole period from the date of his advance to the date, not of the arrival of the 90 days' sight draft, but of the maturity of that draft.

It may happen in the case of a sterling bill drawn on Stockholm that the Swedish drawee happens to have at his disposal a certain quantity of sterling, and he may prefer to pay the bill by means of a sterling cheque for its face value rather than pay kroner. That procedure might be advantageous to him if he had bought the sterling a little time before, and by the time the bill became due kroner had gone up in value. He preferred to use his sterling rather than pay kroner. There would be no reason why the drawer of the bill should not accept the drawee's proposal, for all he desires is to get the face value of the bill, but the collecting bank must first get the assent of the drawer to the proposition. Once a bank has been handed over a bill for collection, it is not authorized to vary its terms in any way whatever, and since the bill is claused " Payable at the drawing rate for demand drafts on London," it had to be paid in that way, unless the assent of the drawer was obtained to vary those terms.

Two sources of difficulty have arisen in recent years in regard to the collection of foreign bills which did not exist before the war. The first has arisen in some continental countries by reason of the idea, widespread among modern governments, that they are superior to the laws of economics. The government has endeavoured by law to alter the rates at which payment was made in respect of bills drawn in sterling, to the advantage of their own nationals. Such attempts have been made in Belgium and Portugal. The rule, as we have stated, is that a bill in sterling had to be paid by that amount of foreign currency which would purchase a draft at sight on London for the full face value of the bill. In Belgium a law was passed to the effect that foreign bills could be paid either in Belgium francs or in the foreign currency in question, at the option of the drawee. In Portugal an attempt was made to evade the rule by decreeing that foreign bills were to be paid at a rate fixed by the Government from time to time. Supposing for example that the market rate on any given day was 50 escudos to the pound ;

the Government might fix the rate at 45; clearly 45 escudos would purchase less sterling than 50, so that the Portuguese drawee paid less than he should have done, and the English drawer received less for his bill than he should have done. One is glad to say that both these attempts failed. A number of protests were made, which in the case of Belgium were effective. In the case of Portugal, shipments simply ceased until the Government was forced to rescind the decree. The second difficulty arises out of more general causes and is not avoidable.[1] Supposing a bill is received by the Swiss banking correspondent of a London bank to whom the bill has been sent by the British drawer for collection. It reaches the Swiss bank at 11 o'clock; the bank sends it out for payment immediately, having of course noted on it the quantity of Swiss francs required to purchase a sight draft on London for the face value of the bill. The drawee, who is somewhere in the country, pays that number of francs, but by the time the francs reach the Swiss collecting bank the rate has altered, and gone against Switzerland, and the number of francs will no longer purchase a sight draft on London for the face value of the bill, but will only purchase a draft for rather less than that amount. The collecting bank has done its duty by sending the bill out immediately it received it, and the drawee has paid the amount of francs for which he was asked, and which at the time he paid them would have purchased a sight draft on London. The drawer, however, gets less than the full face value of the bill, owing to the fact that between 11 o'clock and 3 o'clock there has been a fluctuation in the exchange rates, over which none of the parties concerned had any control. Had the fluctuation been in the other direction, the collecting bank would probably have pocketed the

[1] See the "Banker's Magazine" of November, 1919, on "Foreign Collections' Difficulties."

difference; but as it is, the drawer has to stand the loss.

That is more likely to happen on the Continent than here, because in many parts communications are worse there, and also because, on the Continent, with the exception of Germany, they tend to take things more easily than we do here. Business customs being what they are, it would probably be unreasonable to expect the amount of celerity in collecting drafts which the business man expects from bankers in this country.

The next question is that of interest. Whether or not interest is added to the sum which the drawee has to pay will depend upon whether the bill does or does not contain an interest clause. If it does not, then interest will not come into the question. It may be that the drawer has added interest when making up the face value of the bill, or it may be that for business reasons he does not propose to charge interest. If interest is to be added to the face value of the bill, it must be claused accordingly. The clause will be in this form: "Pay ——— the sum of £—— with interest added hereto at —— per cent. per annum from date hereof to the approximate due date of arrival of remittance in London." The collecting bank on the other side will calculate the approximate date of the arrival of its remittance in London, and will calculate interest for the period between date of the bill and the date of arrival of remittance in London at the rate stated on the bill. This amount of interest will be added to the quantity of currency which the drawee has to pay to the collecting bank on the other side. At what figure the drawer originally fixes the rate will vary in accordance with (*a*) general interest rates, and (*b*) the custom of the particular centre on which the bill is drawn.

The last matter to be mentioned is that a bill may be dishonoured either by non-acceptance or by non-payment. When a bill is dishonoured, the holder must give notice of dishonour to all the parties to the bill whom he intends to hold liable on it, e.g. the drawer and previous endorsers. In the case of a foreign bill, the bill must also be noted and protested, before a notary. The holder can then, if necessary, sue any of these parties to enforce their liability. Sometimes a party is named in a bill to whom it may be presented in the event of dishonour; such party is called the "Reference in case of need" or the "Case of need." When the drawee cannot be found, or refuses to accept, or is legally debarred from accepting —e.g. an infant—another person may with the holder's consent intervene and accept; but in this case the bill must first be protested. Such an acceptance is known as "acceptance for honour" or "acceptance supra protest."

CHAPTER VII

THE BALANCE OF TRADE

Causes of fluctuations in exchange rates—Political events—Speculation—Balance of indebtedness—Invisible exports—Interest on capital invested abroad—Travel—Balance of trade—Effect on exchange rates—Effect of fluctuations in exchange rates on balance of trade—Does a depreciated exchange benefit the export trade ?—Summary of conclusions.

WE can now examine the various factors which cause the fluctuations in rates of exchange. These factors are the same in kind to-day as they were before the war, although very different in degree. They may be grouped under six headings, as follows :

(1) Balance of indebtedness.
(2) Rates of interest.
(3) Political events or rumours with financial reactions.
(4) Speculation.
(5) Loans and credits.
(6) Inflation of currency and credit.

So far as No. 3 is concerned, very little need be said. There have been plenty of examples. One may recall the fluctuations in the Anglo-American Exchange at the time the American Senate was discussing the Peace Treaty, and how the exchange went alternately up and down according as it was believed the Senate would or would not ratify the Treaty. There is a still more recent example in the case of Upper Silesia. One of the greatest of the sudden collapses of the German mark began with a slump of 100 to 200 points, on the arrival in Berlin of the news that this country had agreed to the enforcement of the decision which took a large part of Upper Silesia from Germany and gave it to Poland. The reason was that Silesia is an important mining and industrial area and its loss enormously diminished Germany's wealth and productive ability.

Again, so far as No. 4 is concerned, very little need be said. It is quite evident that when the mark is declining, people who think it is going to decline still further will sell forward, i.e. if the mark is at 800, a man will sell, and buy in when the exchange is at 1,100. The fact that he sells at 800 itself tends to bring the value of the mark down, and when he buys in at 1,100, the mere fact of his buying causes the mark to go up.

The other factors need more detailed analysis.

No. 1, The balance of indebtedness, is made up of five sub-factors:

(*a*) The balance of trade.
(*b*) Invisible exports and imports, such as shipping and insurance services, and
(*c*) Banking and acceptance services.
(*d*) Interest on capital invested abroad.
(*e*) Payments arising out of social intercourse.

(*b*) is simple. It is quite clear that if goods from the United States of America to the West Indies are carried in a British ship, and payment for the freight is made in London, the effect will be to increase *pro tanto* the demand for sterling on the part of the shippers, who will have to expend dollars to buy the sterling.

(*c*) It is also quite clear when the accepting house in London financed the shipment of tea from Canton to Milan, it took a commission for doing so, and the use of these acceptance facilities has therefore increased the demand *pro tanto* for sterling.

(*d*) Suppose a municipality in Brazil raises a loan in this country by offering bonds for subscription. In due course it comes to pay the interest on them. That interest has to be paid either in sterling or in milreis. If in sterling, it means that the municipality has to go into the foreign exchange market and buy sterling, which means an increase in the demand for sterling. If on the other hand the interest is to be paid in milreis, it means that when the bondholders here receive their dividends in milreis, they sell them, thus putting more milreis on the market; in other words, the milreis becomes cheaper. In the past, this country used to draw tribute from all over the world in this way, because in North and South America, and in fact practically all over the world, railways and large undertakings were to a large extent financed by British capital. This is no longer the case to the same extent, because during the war we were compelled to sell a large portion of our best securities in America in order to raise money there.

(*e*) When an English honeymoon couple go to Italy, they have to buy lire to meet their expenses, and that causes the demand for lire, on the part of people who pay for it in sterling, to increase. Similarly, remittances from Irish and Italians in America to people at home cause a demand for sterling or lire on the part of people who buy these currencies with dollars.

(*a*) This is rather more complicated. The balance of trade can of course always be gauged from the Board of Trade returns, which give statistics of imports and exports. The complications arise because not merely does the balance of trade affect the exchanges, but the exchanges themselves have a counter-effect on the balance of trade. Both factors are working at the same time; both are causes, and both are effects. We have to consider separately the effect of each on the other.

The Effect of the Balance of Trade on Exchange Rates.—Clearly, as between country "A" and country "B," an excess of imports over exports in the case of "A" means that "A" will have to accept more bills than it draws; therefore, other things being equal, bills on "A" will be more plentiful than bills on "B," and therefore the price for bills on "A" will be cheaper than the price for bills on "B." We know that the rate on which bankers issue their foreign drafts is determined by the price at which they can buy bills on the country in question, and therefore they will issue drafts on "A" at a cheaper price than bills on "B." That simply means that "A's" rate of exchange will be unfavourable as compared with "B."

In the reverse case, where exports exceed the imports, the same reasoning applies in the reverse direction. In this case, "A's" rate of exchange will be favourable, and "B's" unfavourable.

Such is the reasoning, but these results will only be seen if other things have been equal all along, i.e. if the various other factors, (*b*), (*c*), (*d*), and (*e*), and (2), (3), (4), (5), and (6) have remained unchanged. If for example a country's export trade increased enormously, but at the same time it depreciated its currency very heavily by the issue of paper money, the rates would not go in its favour.[1] All our reasoning is based on the assumption that other things remain equal.

When we come to consider *the counter-effect of the rates of exchange on the balance of trade*, the reasoning is more difficult, for the reason that we have to deal with both the immediate and the secondary effect.

The Immediate Effect.—Take the case where the rate

[1] See the example of Belgium in 1920, quoted in Chapter XI, p. 142.

of exchange between " A " and " B " moves in " A's " favour. That will mean that the price of " A's " currency in terms of " B's " will go up in value: in other words, that the prices quoted by merchants in country " A " are increased automatically to their buyers in " B." If the pound one day is worth 50 francs and the rate moves in favour of England, making the rate 51 francs, and the prices charged by merchants in England remain unchanged, the Frenchman will have to pay 51 francs for an article for which yesterday he was paying 50. The effect is evidently that English export trade will be restricted, because there are always a number of people working on a margin. The buyer may be able to afford an article at 50 francs, but cannot do so at 51 francs; in that case, he does not buy, simply because the rate of exchange has moved in England's favour. Therefore the result of the exchange rates moving in a country's favour is to check the export trade of that country. Following the same line of reasoning conversely, if the rate of exchange goes against England, the effect will be to cheapen English prices to Frenchmen and thereby to increase England's export trade.

So far we have been dealing with immediate effects only. They have led us to the conclusion that an appreciating exchange is a hindrance to the export trade, and a depreciating exchange an advantage to the export trade. And such effects have occurred in actual fact in the case of Germany, where a constantly depreciating exchange has in fact provided an artificial stimulus to the export trade.

But evidently these effects are not the only or the ultimate ones. If a depreciating exchange increases a country's export trade, then clearly the countries with the biggest exports should be Russia, Poland, and Austria. If, again, Germany has been deliberately depressing the exchange in order to pull up her export trade, as some newspapers are never tired of repeating, it is extraordinary that this method of competition never occurred to her or to anyone else before 1914; and still more extraordinary that neither we nor any other industrial nations have followed her example. There have been constant attempts by the German Government and by German financiers to get loans to restore the exchange. Apparently, in spite of the artificial stimulus given to the export trade, no one either in England, in the U.S., or on the Continent really believes that lasting benefit is conferred on a country by a depreciating exchange. The explanation of this apparent contradiction is found in the secondary effects of a depreciating exchange.

The Secondary Effect.—A depreciating exchange means that while exports are made cheaper imports are made dearer. In the case of a manufacturing country, the imports consist chiefly of food and raw materials. A depreciating exchange means an increase in the price of food and raw materials, and therefore an increase in the cost of production. Whether it raises the cost of production to the same extent as the depreciation that has occurred will depend upon a number of things. If there is a depreciation of 25 per cent. in the exchange, it does not necessarily mean that the costs of production will go up 25 per cent. They will go up less or more according to the proportion of food and raw materials imported, and the extent to which salary- and wage-earners are able to force up their remuneration to meet increasing prices. What is certain is that the cost of production will go up. The process is somewhat as follows. When the exchange first depreciates it is a benefit to manufacturers. They are able to raise prices in terms of their own currency to the extent to which the exchange has depreciated without making them dearer to the foreigner. At these new prices they can sell stocks manufactured under the old lower costs of production and pocket the difference. The advantage continues so long as their old stocks last. New goods have to be manufactured out of such stocks of raw material bought at the old prices as remain, and when these are exhausted, out of new stocks bought at the higher prices due to the depreciated exchange. Wages meantime are rising, but in general more slowly than prices, and salaries more slowly than wages. Complications are introduced by the questions as to how quickly raw materials and food produced in the country itself rise in price, and how far rail freights lag behind. But broadly speaking the following would seem to be true. So long as the old stocks of raw materials last, the depreciated exchange still puts a margin into the pockets of manufacturers. Even when they have become exhausted, wages and salaries will in all probability not have risen in the same proportion as prices. To the extent that they will fall short, the advantage to the manufacturer remains, though it may be offset by the friction and strikes to which the readjustment of wages is likely to give rise. Ultimately, assuming the depreciation of the exchange to have stopped, a new equilibrium of prices and wages is reached, and the depreciated exchange ceases to be of benefit to the manufacturer.

It is well to be clear on this point, that the benefit to the industrialists is mainly obtained, not necessarily by their own desire, out of the pockets of the wage-earners, salary-earners, and fixed income-receiving classes of their own country. The incomes of the first rise relatively slowly, those of the second still more slowly, and those of the third not at all. Export prices rise immediately the exchange depreciates, and home prices follow them. Export prices do not necessarily rise to the same extent as the exchange has depreciated—if they did, the depreciation would not be a stimulus to the export trade. Home prices, again, do not necessarily rise to the same extent as export prices; the limitation of the home buying power and governmental regulation, etc., tend to keep them lower.[1] It remains true, however, that the benefit to the export trade conferred by a depreciating exchange is attained mainly at the cost of the middle and working classes.[2] These are the people who pay the artificial premium put on the German export trade by the decline of the mark.

It may be added that a portion of the premium is paid by speculators who have bought marks; but as against this are other speculators who have sold marks forward.

Subject to these considerations, a depreciating exchange is an advantage to the export trade, but it is a lasting advantage only so long as it continues to depreciate. In other words, the benefit is that, not of a depreciated exchange, but of a depreciating exchange.[3]

But the examples of Poland, Austria, and Russia show that a constantly depreciating exchange ceases at some point to be a benefit even to the export trade. At what point it seems impossible to say theoretically; certainly the point varies in the case of different countries, according, *inter alia,* to the degree to which it is industrial, to the strength of its organized workers, to the extent to which it is self-sufficing in regard to food and raw materials. The history of Germany in the near future may throw light on this question. Evidently what happens is something of this sort: A state of things is reached where the wage-earners of a country get thoroughly discontented, because they have continually increasing wages which mean nothing, on account of the

[1] See Chapter XII as to the gap between home and export prices, especially p. 155.

[2] For a comparison of the rises of (*a*) prices, (*b*) wages, and (*c*) salaries, in Germany, concurrently with the decline in value of the mark, see p. 165, footnote.

[3] Mr. F. W. Hirst, in "Common Sense," appears to have been the first to draw the distinction clearly in this form.

increased prices. Neither they nor still less the salaried classes can keep up with the increased cost of living. The purchasing power of the other section of the middle classes (those who live on fixed incomes) has long since disappeared. The result is that with the rising prices the home purchasing power collapses. Foreign markets become satiated with cheap goods, or keep them out by tariffs and prohibitions. The depreciating exchange meantime has so increased the cost of manufactured articles that to replace worn out or obsolete machinery, and to carry stocks, requires such enormous capital that business enterprise is discouraged. The increase in the prices of manufactured goods, among other effects, causes the point to be approached where farmers will no longer find it worth while to produce a surplus above their own requirements, the more so as food prices will probably have been kept artificially low for the sake of the town workers. The only remedy is a State subsidy. The finances of the State become hopeless, for taxes fixed at the old currency values will not meet the expenditure determined by the new. As a result of all these conditions, and in turn intensifying them, discontent and loss of confidence grow to an extent which imperils the fabric of the State and of society itself. The rest is politics.

To sum up these conclusions:

(1) The following generalizations are subject to the disturbing influence of tariffs, import and export prohibitions and restrictions, subsidies, etc.

(2) A depreciated exchange exercises its full benefit on the export trade only so long as stocks of manufactured goods last.

(3) The benefit is obtained by industrialists and merchants at the expense mainly of wage- and salary-earners and people with fixed incomes in their own country.

(4) In this sense it remains beneficial, though to a less degree, so long as stocks of raw material last.

(5) After these two kinds of stocks are exhausted, it is only beneficial until wages and salaries have risen in proportion to prices.

(6) When a new equilibrium of wages, salaries, and prices has been set up, the benefit disappears entirely, except in so far as real wages and salaries may have been permanently lowered, unless the exchange continues to depreciate.

(7) The foregoing benefits are liable to be offset by (*a*) the industrial friction, (*b*) financial difficulties, (*c*) the social and political complications which a depreciating exchange brings in its train.

(8) There is a point at which the factors mentioned under (7) are brought to such a pitch of strength by the exhaustion of internal, and the satiation of external, purchasing power, that even a depreciating exchange ceases to be a benefit to the export trade, but becomes dangerous to political, social, and economic stability.

It may happen, however, that the process of depreciating ceases, by reason of the fact that the internal and external influences which have been adversely affecting the currency cease to be operative. What would happen in that case we shall see later.[1]

[1] See page 182.

CHAPTER VIII

LOANS AND CREDITS

Effect of international loans and credits on exchange rates—Example—Effect of raising a loan, of paying interest, of repayment—The "pegging" of the dollar rate during the war—How the American debt was created—The Stock market and the exchanges.

WE next have to consider the fourth of the six factors which influence exchange rates: international loans and credits. Such loans and credits may be either private or public. It may be for example that a merchant in Brazil seeks accommodation in London, or it may be that the Brazilian Government floats a loan in London. We may take a case which combines the features of both in order to show how it works: the case of a Brazilian municipality raising a loan in London through a London financial house. The loan may be made in one of three forms. In the first place it may be made through an issuing house, i.e. one of those houses which specialize in placing foreign bonds on the market. The house sells the bonds on behalf of the municipality, people here will subscribe for and receive the bonds, paying the issuing house sterling therefor, and the latter places the money to the credit of the municipality in a London joint-stock bank. Let us say the loan has been raised in order to build a local tramway. The contract for rolling stock, rails, overhead, etc., is placed by the municipality with a well-known British firm. When the goods are ready to be shipped, the municipality instructs the bank which holds its funds to pay the amount to the suppliers' invoice against shipping documents. The effect of the raising of the loan has been to enable the Brazilian municipality to pay for the British manufactures it requires by utilizing British credit facilities. Another way in which the same end might be attained would be by way of a merchant bank. In this instance one of the London merchant bankers agrees with a Brazilian municipality to accept bills drawn upon themselves up to a certain amount. The material is ordered, the contractors draw on the merchant bankers, and the latter pay. In a third instance the loan may be issued through an accepting house: in this case the accepting house gives authority to the municipality to draw upon themselves up to a certain amount. In this case the credit is a blank credit. The municipality have the right to draw on the accepting house up to let us say £10,000. When the material is shipped, the amount the municipality has to pay through its London agents is £8,500. The agents draw £9,000, the accepting house accept the bill, the agents discount it with a London bank, and pay the suppliers out of the balance thereby created.

In all three cases, the effect is that a Brazilian purchaser gets goods for which at the time he pays out of funds lent to him for the purpose by people in London. As a result, he is indebted to people in England, either bondholders, merchant bankers, or an accepting house. The effect of these credit operations clearly is that the municipality will not have to go into the foreign exchange market and buy sterling bills, whereas if it had not had credit, it would have had to do so. In the ordinary way the municipality would have had to spend milreis in purchasing sterling in order to pay the contractors; as it is, they have not had to expend milreis at all. There is therefore less of a demand from Brazil for sterling than there would otherwise have been: the effect of the issuing of this loan is to keep the Brazilian exchange more favourable to Brazil than it would have been had it not been issued. Exactly the same effect would be produced if instead of the municipality the borrower had been any ordinary merchant in Brazil, or the Brazilian Government itself, desirous perhaps of borrowing money from our Government to pay for warships which were being built for them in the shipyards of Great Britain. To generalize, the effect of the giving of credits is to tend to make the exchange favourable to the country which gets the credit.

When the time comes for the interest to be paid on the loan, the effect on the exchanges is exactly opposite. The interest on the bonds may be payable either in sterling or milreis, but the effect will be the same in either case. If payable in sterling, the municipality will have to buy sterling bills in order to create a balance for itself in London out of which it can pay the bondholders. That means the demand from Brazil for sterling bills will be greater than before, and the price of them will rise. If the interest is payable in milreis, it means that a number of bondholders in England will receive drafts in milreis, which they will sell to their banks, and the banks will sell on the foreign exchange market. Therefore there will be a larger supply of milreis than before, and the price of milreis will be less. The exchange will tend to go against Brazil just as in the case when the interest was payable in sterling.

The creation of loans will favour the exchange of the debtor country. The payment of interest will favour the exchange of the creditor country.

The effect of the repayment of the loans in question is similar. In the case of the loans made by the merchant bankers and the accepting house, the period of the loan would be relatively short, and the loan known as a short-dated credit; in the case of the bonds, it would probably be a long-dated loan. In either case, the effects of repayment on the exchange are the same in principle as when the interest had to be paid, i.e. the municipality once more had to go into the market and buy sterling in order to repay the English creditors.

Before the war, London financial houses did a very great deal of this sort of business. American, Australian, Canadian, and South American municipalities, railroads, and public utility companies all made a habit of financing their requirements in London. The commission obtained on this business was an element of considerable profit to this country, and the interest obtained from capital invested abroad was an item which swelled the income of this country to the tune of about £400,000,000 annually. Now, an important part of that has gone, because the best of our foreign securities were sold during the war in the United States. New York, again, has become a better centre than London for raising loans, because the resources of the United States were not lessened by the war, and the dollar possesses that certain convertibility into gold which before the war was the property of the pound alone. The financing of Canadian public and private requirements, i.e. municipal loans and the capital issues of limited companies, has largely passed from London to New York.

The floating of loans and the giving of credits was the means whereby Britain assisted her allies financially during the war, and whereby the U.S. assisted Britain. It was the means whereby, before the U.S. entered the war, the dollar exchange was fixed at the figure of 4·76½, or, as it was called, "pegged." The principle was that payments for food and munitions supplied by U.S. firms to this country were made out of dollar funds raised in the United States, so that no dollars had to be bought, and therefore these British purchases did not for the time being produce any effect on the exchange. The details of this pegging are worthy of examination, as they are very instructive in regard to the operation of this part of exchange machinery.

Towards the end of 1914, the decline of the export trade of the Allied belligerent countries and their necessity to import, at a time when their resources were being progressively devoted to the war, caused the neutral, and especially the American, exchanges to move against them. In September, 1915, the dollar was down to 4·75 and it was clear that, in the absence of preventive measures, it would decline further by reason of the huge payments necessitated by imports of food and munitions. It had become evident that a war policy based on unlimited military commitments would require, in order to pay for imports of food and munitions in the absence of any considerable exports, the selling of oversea investments and the creation of a foreign debt. The alternative was to limit English military participation and to rely, apart from the very considerable armies already raised at that time, on naval and economic means. The former course was chosen. Loans were raised in the United States and foreign investments were sold in New York to provide funds. By this means the necessity of buying dollars to pay for food and munitions was avoided for the time and the dollar remained at the figure it had reached, 4·76½.

At first, British loans in America were raised in somewhat the same manner as, in the imaginary example set out earlier, the Brazilian municipality raised its loan in England. They were raised through the firm of J. P. Morgan & Co., and out of the funds so provided, payment was made for British imports of food and munitions. As time went on, and the destruction of the belligerent countries' resources became evident to the neutral world, a feeling arose in the U.S. that such loans should not be issued without some security behind them, and a regulation was issued to that effect. This necessitated that when England raised loans in the U.S. (we are still dealing of course with the period prior to the entry of the U.S. into the war) collateral securities had to be deposited. This gave rise to what was known in England as the "Dollar Securities Scheme." Residents in England were invited to surrender to the British Treasury securities of various kinds named in the Treasury circulars. The Treasury promised either to return them the securities or to pay the owners their market value; in the meantime the owners would receive the interest due, but the Treasury had the right to dispose of the securities as it thought fit. The securities covered by that scheme were such as the U.S. financial community would accept as security for loans, and consisted, broadly speaking, of the choicest of the American (U.S., South American, and Canadian) bonds held in England. Finding that the voluntary appeal to owners of listed securities to surrender them did not have the effect of mobilizing all the securities available, the Treasury in 1916 instituted a penal income tax on the income from securities not handed to the Treasury. Finally, the handing over of the listed securities was made compulsory. The securities so obtained by the Treasury were either sold in New York or deposited as collateral for loans in the U.S. It was when England was approaching a point at which loans had been issued to the full extent to which the Americans were willing to lend on the security of these bonds that Mr. Bonar Law made his famous declaration, early in 1917, that "our resources are not unlimited." What would have been the course of events had not the U.S. entered the war at this point is of course one of those "might-have-beens" which fascinate the historical imagination. The considerations at issue in the first months of 1917 were not merely financial, but economic; unless the food, raw materials, and munitions which America alone could supply in adequate quantities could be obtained, the war would have had to be ended. Credits could not be obtained without security, and there was no more security to give, with the possible exception of the cession of the West Indian Islands. Without credits, the sterling used in purchasing dollars would have declined rapidly in value, and with every decline the imports would automatically have become dearer. As it was clear that only by virtue of a greatly superior supply of food and munitions (as well as men) could Germany be defeated, the end could not, it would seem, have been long delayed.

The entry of the U.S. into the war solved the problem by altering the manner in which loans in America were raised. Hitherto the money had come from private individuals in the U.S.; henceforth the loans were made by the U.S. Government. These loans were made chiefly to Britain, Britain re-lending the money to her Allies.

The U.S. Government paid U.S. manufacturers and grain exporters for the goods and food supplied to the European belligerents, debiting therefore the British Government, which in turn debited its Allies in the cases where the goods and food were supplied to them. The position to-day,[1] broadly speaking, is that Britain owes the United States about £978,000,000, and is owed a larger sum by her former Allies and her Dominions.

The dollar exchange remained at the figure of 4·76½, there being nothing to move it, until March, 1919, when it was "unpegged," i.e. the British Treasury announced that no further steps would be taken to stabilize it.

In the case of the Central Powers, which for practical purposes consisted of Germany, the problem was different. Germany was, save in certain limited directions, barred from export and import, and conducted the war from her own resources. The problems of the foreign exchanges only arose in the case of the limited directions

[1] July, 1922. For details of the position, see p. 185.

in which export and import was possible—Holland, Sweden, Denmark, and, for a time, Rumania. In these cases credits were arranged, and liquidated by the export of stipulated goods, such as coal.[1]

Connected with the subject of the influence of international loans on the exchanges is that of the relationship between the stock market and the exchanges. The purchase of the securities of a foreign country is in effect a loan to that country. When the British Treasury sold dollar securities in the United States, Americans were in effect repaying former loans. When a British investor buys French war-loan or shares in a Spanish mine, he is in effect putting money into France or Spain. If the securities he buys were previously held in the country of origin, the former holder will have to be paid in francs or pesetas, and these will ultimately have to be bought by sterling. If the securities purchased were already held in Britain, the purchaser is in effect renewing a previous loan; if the purchaser, instead of being an Englishman, had been a Frenchman or a Spaniard, the securities would have been sent back to France or Spain, and the purchaser there would have had to buy sterling in order to pay for them. In the first case, a demand from London for francs or pesetas is set up which did not exist before; in the second case, a potential demand for sterling is prevented from coming into existence. The effect in either case is to tend to influence the exchange against sterling, i.e. against the purchasing country. The position may be viewed as an import of securities [2] into Britain, which like other imports has to be paid for and therefore tends to send the exchange against the importing country.

The stock market and the foreign exchanges act and

[1] Details are given in Helferrich: "Der Weltkrieg" (II^er Band, "Vom Kriegsausbruch bis zum uneingeschränkten U-Bootkrieg").

[2] The conception is that of Mr. Hartley Withers.

react on each other. If the tendency is for, e.g., Brazilian securities to go up in value, then the value of Brazilian currency will tend to go up with them, i.e. the number of milreis to be surrendered for one pound will go down. The reason is that a rise in the price indicates the activities of buyers on this side, who will require milreis to remit in payment for the securities newly absorbed by the English market. Similarly, if the Brazilian exchange is unfavourable to Brazil, quotations for Brazilian securities worth so many milreis will naturally tend to go down. In the ordinary way, that would be a good time to buy Brazilian securities, and such purchases, in their turn, would tend to set the exchange right.

During 1919 to 1921, the low exchange rates of a good many continental countries have caused a good deal of capital to flow into them by way of the purchase of their industrial securities. The price of German, Austrian, Hungarian, Czech, and Polish industrial securities has advanced on the heels of their falling exchanges, but has not always kept up with them. When it fell behind, these securities looked cheap to foreign buyers, and capital flowed in accordingly. Thus English and French capital has gone into Austria, Hungary, and Czecho-Slovakia; French capital into Poland; English and Dutch capital into Germany. Latterly, the losses sustained by English industrialists in the slump following 1920, together with the increasing evidence of instability in Central Europe, have reacted against this investment of capital abroad.

Another interesting illustration of the relation between the exchanges and the stock market is supplied by the following advice given in May, 1920, by a well-known firm of investment bankers in London to those of their clients who had sums on deposit in France in francs, representing money that was owing to them. These clients had left the money in France hoping that the exchange would from France's point of view improve, but had at length come to the opinion that no such improvement was likely. They were accordingly faced with the question how best to deal with these franc balances without absolutely cutting the loss by exchanging them for sterling at the then ruinous rate of exchange. They were advised by the investment bankers "to invest the amount in francs in some good foreign Government Bond, quoted in Paris, interest and capital of which are payable not only in francs, but in sterling, and possibly some other currency, such as Brazilian Government or Argentine Government Bonds or Stocks. Of course, the franc quotations of these Bonds bear some relation to the present depreciated value of the franc, but by converting francs into such Bonds, the holder insures himself against any further depreciation, secures a high rate of interest (payable in francs or sterling as he desires) on the capital outstanding, and gives to his capital mobility, for he can at any time bring the Bonds over to this country, where they can be sold for sterling without being affected by the French rate of exchange; and at the same time, he retains the possibility of adding to his capital in francs in the event of the quotation of the foreign Bonds rising in Paris."

CHAPTER IX

THE SILVER EXCHANGES

The Eastern exchanges—Influence of the price of silver—Rise in price of silver during and after the war, its causes and its effect on the silver exchanges—Rupee, lac and crore—Gold exchange standard—India's trade balance—India Council drafts—Reverse Councils—The rupee and the rise in silver—Indian currency measures of 1920—Effects—Later decline in value of rupee—Rate of exchange for conversion of legal damages in currency into sterling.

THE Eastern exchanges are subject to all the ordinary factors governing the movement of exchange rates, named at the beginning of Chapter VI, and in addition they vary with the price of silver. They are the exchanges of the silver-using countries, and there are therefore in these cases no pars of exchange[1] and no gold points. In the last instance, silver, and not gold, is shipped for what it will fetch. Purchasing Eastern exchange is really purchasing a claim to silver. Hence these exchanges fluctuate according, not only to the general factors influencing exchange fluctuations which we have examined, but also according to the price of silver, in terms of, before the war, gold, and now, of our paper currency. The price of silver plus or minus shipping charges roughly fixes the rate above and below which the Eastern exchanges will not go. That statement of course is subject to the very important exception of India, which is governed by special con-

[1] Except in the case of Japan, where the Yen is on a gold basis.

ditions. During and for some time after the war, the price for silver went up very considerably, and the Eastern exchanges appreciated accordingly. The rise in the price of silver was due to both the decrease in the supply and the increase in the demand. The decrease in the supply, due directly or indirectly to the war, can be seen by comparing the figures for the total world production of silver in 1913 and 1918. Between those dates it had declined by something over 18 per cent. The increase in the demand was brought about by various factors, of which we may name three as the chief:

(1) Silver, and of course paper, was required to take the place of gold which went out of circulation in this and other belligerent countries; while the need for silver as a medium of circulation, independently of its replacing gold, was increased in those parts of the world which were blessed with a British Army of Occupation, such as Egypt and Mesopotamia.

(2) During the war period, India and China absorbed considerable quantities, which were hoarded. The native likes to keep his wealth in the form of silver, just as some people like to keep theirs in the form of jewellery.

(3) The price of silver was sent up by the depreciation of the medium in which the price was being reckoned, e.g. English currency. The decline in the value of English currency during the war was shown, *inter alia*, by the increase in prices: silver is a commodity like everything else, and as the prices of other things went up, so did the price of silver.

The operation of those various factors in raising the price of silver was very marked. In 1914 its price (June 30th) was 26d. per ounce. In October, 1919, the price reached 64d. per ounce; in February, 1920, it went to 89½d. per ounce. We shall find that the increase in the value of the Eastern exchange which took place was roughly parallel. The Chinese tael for example in 1914 averaged 2s. 4d., in October, 1919, it had risen to 6s. 4d., and in February, 1920, to 9s. 3d. The percentage increases were thus:

	Silver	Tael
1914 to Oct., 1919 - -	167	171½
1914 to Feb., 1920 - -	273	296½

from which the close correspondence between the rise in value of silver and of the tael is evident. The same correspondence was observed later in 1920, when the price of silver and the value of the tael declined. During 1920, in fact, the value of the tael fluctuated between 3s. 10½d. and 9s. 3d. The Hong-Kong dollar followed a similar course. The uncertainty which these fluctuations brought into Far Eastern and similarly to the Indian trade is obvious: the enormous rise in the purchasing power of these coins induced purchasers to order goods far in excess of what the market could take. Frequently when the time came for payment, the currencies had declined in value. Sometimes, as in a number of cases in India, the goods were not taken up, and had to be sold for what they would fetch, after having accumulated huge charges for warehousing and interest. However disposed of, they choked the market, and when the slump came in the wake of the price boom of early 1920, they hindered the market's recovery.

Another interesting example of the relation between the price of silver and the exchange values of Eastern currencies, and the connexion of the two with the stock and share market, was observed about the turn of the year 1919–20, when there was a sensational rise in the shares of one of the large German banks—the Deutsch-Asiatische Bank. The reason was that the bank, as its name suggests, operated largely in China and Japan. The increase in the value of silver brought about an increase in the value of Chinese and Japanese currencies, and that meant an increase in the value of the property and funds owned by the bank; hence the shares of the bank were considered to be of more value.

In India the standard coin is the rupee. A lac is 100,000 rupees, a crore is 100 lacs. The rupee itself is silver, but there was a gold exchange standard. The rupee was an example of a currency that was a sort of "half-way house"[1] between convertibility into gold and non-convertibility. Anyone who had sovereigns in India had the right to change those sovereigns into rupees at the rate of 15 to the pound, but the converse was not true. There was no obligation on the Indian Mint to give sovereigns in exchange for rupees. Such was the Mint position of Indian currency in pre-war times. Before the basis of Indian currency was altered in 1920, the rupee had to contain 165 grains of fine silver. As one ounce of standard silver contains 444 grains of fine silver, it follows that one rupee equalled $\frac{165}{444}$ of the price per ounce of standard silver. From that we get Clare's rule[2] for determining the approximate sight exchange of the rupee from the price of standard silver. The rule is: The approximate sight exchange can be got from the price of standard silver by adding $\frac{3}{8}$d. to $\frac{3}{8}$th of the price per ounce of silver; thus: supposing the price of standard silver to be 40d. per ounce, $\frac{3}{8}$ths of that is 15d., and if we add $\frac{3}{8}$d., we get 1s. 3$\frac{3}{8}$d., which would be the approximate sight exchange when silver is 40d. That rule worked under pre-war conditions, though it was never intended to be more than approximate.

The trade balance was nearly always in favour of India. Exports more than counterbalanced imports to such an extent that it provided a surplus over and above all the payments which India had to make, which can be summarized under four headings:

[1] The term was applied by Mr. Hartley Withers.

[2] "The A.B.C. of the Foreign Exchanges."

(1) For imports.
(2) For interest on government and railway loans.
(3) For I.C.S. pensions.
(4) For the upkeep of the India Office in London.

The actual machinery by which remittances to and from India are made is also worthy of a brief examination. Remittances to India are made by means of India Council drafts. They are drafts sold in London to merchants who have to remit to India, and consist of bills drawn on the Indian Treasuries and payable at various places in India in rupees. They are obtainable both in the form of deferred transfers and immediate telegraphic transfers. The deferred transfers are cheaper than the telegraphic transfer by, as a rule, $\frac{1}{32}$d. per rupee.[1] The difference represents interest for the period which elapses before the buyer of the deferred transfer, who has paid sterling for it, is credited with the rupees. Remittances in the other direction, i.e. from India to England, are made either by ordinary sterling drafts or by "Reverse Councils." These Reverse Councils are sterling drafts sold by the Indian Government, payable in London; they are sold when the demand for sterling drafts is large and pre-war they were sold at a fixed price which was 1/3$\frac{29}{32}$d. per rupee. The fact that the Indian Government was always willing to sell Reverse Councils at that fixed rate, determined, as it were, the lower gold point. The means whereby the Indian Government was able to sell Reverse Councils were provided by a gold backing in London, in the form of gold reserves which the Bank of England held in London for the Indian Government. The combination of a trade balance favourable to India and the right to exchange sovereigns into rupees enabled the rupee, although not based on gold, to be maintained at a fixed exchange rate with gold—at the figure of 1s. 3$\frac{29}{32}$d.

[1] Spalding, "Foreign Exchange and Foreign Bills," p. 134.

During and after the war, the increase in the price of silver put the Indian Government in a very difficult position. With the rupee at 16d., the cost of the silver in it to anyone who melted it down would be $(16 \times \frac{444}{165})$d. per oz. = 43d. per oz. If therefore the price of standard silver went above that figure, then the obvious tendency would be for rupees to be melted down and sold as silver bullion, which would create a recurrent shortage of currency in India; on the other hand, to coin fresh rupees at the legal rate of 15 per pound when silver was costing so much more would have meant a huge loss to the Indian Government. To get out of that difficulty they adopted three palliative measures and then in 1919 a fourth measure, which amounted to an entire alteration of the basis of Indian currency. The three measures were:

(1) They prohibited the import and export of silver.

(2) They increased the price of council drafts to 2s. 4d., that is, they made the rupee more valuable.

(3) They imported gold at the rate of 11 rupees to the pound and then sold it in India.

The last measure amounted really to this: they induced the Indian population to invest its wealth in gold. A favourable trade balance and the increase in the price of silver were thus partly offset by India importing gold. As these there measures did not surmount the difficulty, they adopted the fourth measure, which amounted to changing the basis of Indian currency. In February, 1920, the Indian Government fixed a rupee at one-tenth of a gold sovereign. The iffect of that decision provided an interesting lesson in exchange economics. Before this altereation a rupee was valued at 2s - 4d; after being fixed at one-tenth of a gold covereign, it jumped to 2s. 9d. That showed a depreciation in the pound. It showed that gold prices were something different to prices in English paper currency. The amount of the jump, practically 18 per cent., represented the amount by which paper prices were higher than gold prices. As a matter of fact, at that time if we had worked out the depreciation of the English pound on the basis of the then price of gold in terms of Bradburys, we would have found that round about 20 per cent. was the actual extent of the depreciation of the paper pound in terms of gold.

The idea underlying the decision to fix the rupee at one-tenth of a gold sovereign was that when sterling recovered its parity with gold, the value of the rupee would have been permanently increased. In effect, however, that reasoning did not hold good. Since that time the rupee has fallen considerably in value. The Indian importer who had the pleasure of seeing the rupee go up to 2s. 4d. and then jump further to 2s. 9d. and was then assured by the Government that the increase in value was to be permanent, found that nothing of the sort was the case. That was due to two factors. In the first place, silver did not maintain the price it reached—the price of silver in July, 1922, for example was 35⅛d. as against 88¼d. in February, 1920. That was one cause of the decline in value. The second was that the Indian trade balance went against India. Into the causes of that we cannot here go in detail, but may name two causes: one was that India bought heavily following the termination of the war, and of course had to pay for those imports; and another cause was that one of India's largest pre-war markets for tea, Russia, disappeared from the market for an indefinite period. As a result of the swinging-over of the trade balance, and the decline in the price of silver, the Indian rupee slumped very considerably. It has not even been maintained at 2s. paper, let alone 2s. gold. In July, 1922, its value measured in terms of the paper pound was 1s. 3⅝d.

The decline in the value of the rupee led in 1921 to unexpected and unpleasant results for British exporters to India. A number of Indian importers, upset by the general decline in prices which had occurred since they had placed their orders in 1920—a decline intensified for them by the drop in the value of the rupee—and themselves perhaps not uninfluenced by political propaganda, repudiated their contracts and refused to take up the goods they had bought. Actions claiming damages for breach of contract were brought in Indian courts by British exporters, and substantial damages were awarded. The damages were assessed in the only currency in which an Indian court could assess them—in rupees. The actual payment however, being made to persons in England, had to be made in sterling, which the defendants would have to purchase and remit. The question therefore arose : At what rate were the rupee damages to be converted into sterling ? At the rate ruling on the day when the breach of contract, in respect of which the damages were awarded, took place ; or at the rate ruling on the day when judgment was delivered ? Between these two dates the rupee had declined in value in terms of sterling. The second date would therefore mean the payment to the successful plaintiffs of a lesser sterling amount than the first. Naturally the English plaintiffs argued for the first rate, the Indian defendants for the second.

Unfortunately for the English plaintiffs, some cases had already been decided in the English courts,[1] in which the rule was laid down that the rate at which damages, awarded in one country to plaintiffs domiciled in another, were to be converted was the rate ruling on the date of judgment. These cases were King's Bench cases, and therefore without the authority attaching to an

[1] *Di Ferdinando* v. *Simon Smits & Co.* (L.R., 1920, Vol. II, K.B. & P., Part VIII) was the chief of these cases.

Appeal case; but the rule was laid down sufficiently clearly to induce the English plaintiffs to accept the Indian defendants' views without taking the matter further.

Into the legal grounds for the King's Bench decisions in question it is unnecessary to go. It may, however, be remarked that the practical effect of these decisions was inequitable, in that they brought about a state of affairs in which a party to a contract for goods, of which the price had declined before delivery could be made, might find it cheaper to refuse to take the goods and have damages awarded against him than to take up the goods; because the damages awarded against the defaulter were automatically diminished, at the time he had to pay them, by the decline in value of the currency in which they were assessed. It might be, that is, more profitable to break a contract than to perform it, a state of things which has induced some buyers to break contracts or to refuse to take up goods unless extortionate allowances were made by the sellers.

CHAPTER X

INTEREST RATES: BANK RATE AND THE EXCHANGES

Interest rates and the exchanges under pre-war conditions—Discount market—Money Market—Various money rates—Effect on exchanges of fluctuations in market rate—How Bank of England's manipulation of bank rate formerly turned exchanges in our favour—Why this manipulation no longer produces its former effect.

WE have now to consider the influence of rates of interest on exchange rates. The importance of the interplay of interest rates and exchange rates is that on this interplay depended the whole regulating machinery of the exchanges as they existed before the war. That regulating machinery was bank rate, i.e. the rate at which the Bank of England will discount approved bills of exchange of three months' maturity. It was by manipulating its rate that the Bank of England turned the exchanges in our favour, and attracted gold from abroad at a time when without such manipulation the exchanges would have gone against us, and gold would have left the country. This regulating machinery depended for its effect on the interplay of interest rates and exchange rates.

It is necessary to bear in mind that the description of this interplay immediately following refers to the pre-war exchanges. The machinery does not work to-day in the same way or with the same reliability and effect as it did before the war. Nevertheless, it is the only machinery in existence, and we have to examine how it worked in pre-war times when it was effective, if we are to understand why conditions to-day prevent it from producing the result it formerly did. Since, then, we are speaking of pre-war times, we have to remember that when in this chapter we speak of rates fluctuating, we mean fluctuating in the pre-war sense, i.e. round about par and between the gold points. Thus if we have the Anglo-French exchange in our mind, we are thinking of rates fluctuating between about 25·15 and 25·29, about ·07 on either side of par. We are dealing with very slight fluctuations. Further, it is essential to remember that we are thinking in terms of a currency which was convertible into gold. We are talking about the days before the coming of the currency note, and dealing with the time when the only paper currency in existence in this country consisted of bank-notes, cheques, and bills of exchange; with a time in which such paper currency as existed was convertible into gold. Another way to express the same fact is to say that at that time the volume of our currency was limited in a sense in which it is not limited now. When we speak therefore of certain factors reducing the supply of bills on the market, it means that those factors were reducing the volume of currency. It was possible in those days to increase and diminish the volume of our currency by the manipulation of interest rates. To-day it is not possible to the same degree. Limited fluctuations in the value of a currency convertible into gold: such were the conditions under which what we are about to say held true.

Keeping firmly in mind the fact that the price at which a banker will issue a draft in foreign currency is determined by the price at which he can buy bills in that currency, it is evident that the way in which rates of interest will affect exchange rates is by influencing the price of bills. The organization by means of which bills are exchanged for cash is the money market, and it is therefore necessary to examine in outline its structure and functions. The business of the money market consists in exchanging cash for short period promises to pay. These promises are in the form of bills of exchange. Bills are the commodity in which the money market deals. Ordinary merchants dealing in goods are the producers of bills, as we saw in Chapter IV; the joint-stock banks are the consumers. The intermediaries between the two, the dealers in bills, are the bill-brokers and discount houses. This does not mean that the joint-stock banks do not buy bills direct from the ordinary mercantile holder; they do so buy; but they do so only incidentally, as one only of their many activities. The specialized dealers in bills, the bill-brokers and discount houses on the other hand, do nothing else but buy and sell bills, and from them quotations can always be obtained. The bill-brokers and discount houses, together with the accepting houses or merchant bankers and the London offices of British oversea banks, constitute the "discount market"; and the discount market, together with the joint-stock banks and the Bank of England, constitutes the money market.

How bills of exchange originate and come into the money market we have already seen in Chapter IV. In the case of the bill drawn by Chung Ling Soo on Steinfelds, it will be remembered that the manager of the Canton branch of a British bank trading overseas made an advance to Chung Ling Soo against the bill before acceptance. When the bill has arrived in London and been accepted by Steinfelds, the London office of the bank, if they do not wish to hold it till maturity, will sell it to a discount house. The difference between the London discount rate and the rate at which the Canton manager made the advance represents profit to the bank. Before dealing with the bill-brokers and discount houses, it will be well to be clear as to the ultimate consumers of bills—the joint-stock banks. Why can the banks be relied on by the bill-brokers to buy bills? The reason is this: The outstanding considerations in English banking policy are to keep resources liquid and at the same time to earn interest on them. Apart from the general desirability of keeping resources liquid, since a bank's liabilities are payable on demand (current accounts) or at seven days' notice (deposit accounts) there are certain times of the year at which a bank is particularly in need of ready cash. One such time is the end of December, when, as we all know, there is a certain amount of "window-dressing" in order that the banks' balance sheets may present a favourable appearance in the sense that there is plenty of ready cash available. Another time the banks require particularly large cash resources is during the months of February and March, when clients are drawing large cheques in order to meet income tax. The banks therefore are faced with the necessity of earning interest on money deposited with them in such a manner that a large proportion of that money can be turned into cash at a moment's notice, or better still, will turn itself automatically into cash within a definite time. The way the bank fulfils these two requirements is by:

(*a*) Investing its money in bills of exchange.

(*b*) Lending money at call or short notice.

A bill of exchange will automatically fall due for payment on a certain date, and if it is a good bill, i.e. has good names upon it, it will automatically turn itself into cash on that date. If therefore a bank knows it will require a large amount of cash by a certain date, it buys in from bill-brokers or discount houses a sufficient number of bills of exchange maturing on that date. It thereby secures the certainty of having cash on the date when cash is required and also earns the difference between the face value of the bill, which it receives on maturity, and the amount the bank itself gave for the bill. An example will show that a bank buying a bill with good names on it is sure to make a moderate but certain profit. Take the case of the three months' bill for £100 mentioned in Chapter IV, which the bank, deducting the market rate of discount for three months' trader bills, $5\frac{1}{2}$ per cent. per annum, bought for £98 12s. 6d. The money employed by the banker in buying it is money deposited with him by a customer, on which he has to pay the customer interest. On the same day that trade bills were quoted in the Press at 5 per cent. to $5\frac{1}{2}$ per cent., the Bankers' deposit rate was quoted at $3\frac{1}{2}$ per cent. per annum. The banker has to pay interest at $3\frac{1}{2}$ per cent. per annum on the money deposited with him, which he employed in buying the bill. The sum which the banker had to expend is therefore £98 12s. 6d. plus interest on that at $3\frac{1}{2}$ per cent.

$$= £98\ 12s.\ 6d.\ \text{plus}\ \frac{98{\cdot}625 \times 7 \times 1}{100 \times 2 \times 4}$$
$$= £98\ 12s.\ 6d.\ \text{plus}\ 17s.$$
$$= £99\ 9s.\ 6d.$$

As his total incomings, i.e. the face value of the bill when it matures, are £100, he makes a profit of 10s. 6d. on a transaction of £100 in three months. His profit is at the rate of 2 per cent. per annum.

In fact, his profit is greater, for he would not have to pay interest on the whole of the money. A large quantity of the funds at a banker's disposal do not consist of money placed with him on deposit, but of current accounts, on which he does not pay interest at deposit rate. So in point of fact his expenses are not equal to the figure stated and his profit is correspondingly greater. Moreover, a banker cannot make a loss on the transaction, for deposit rates are normally lower than discount rates. For the banker, such a transaction—always assuming a good bill, and bankers touch no others—shows a moderate and certain profit, and assures that, on a definite date, so much of his assets will automatically turn itself into cash. It is of course true that if discount rates went down and the banker desired to sell the bill, he might have to sell it for less than he gave for it. But banks do not buy bills for resale, but by way of short-dated investment for their funds, and customarily hold them till maturity.

We also said that banks employ a proportion of their funds in loans at call or at seven days' notice. These loans are made to a large extent to the bill-brokers from whom the banks customarily buy their bills of exchange, and such loans are known collectively as "loans to the short loan market," which is so called because the period of the loan is short. The banks also make short loans to stockbrokers and other parties, but in the greatest measure their loans at call and short notice are made to bill-brokers. It is natural to ask: Why do not the banks buy direct from the people who have bills to sell, instead of financing bill merchants to do the business for them? The answer is that there is just as much or as little justification for the existence of a bill-broker as there is for that of any other middleman. Bill-brokers who specialize in inland bills make it their business to have in their portfolios bills of the kind and maturity which the banks favour. Those who specialize in foreign currency bills make it their business to know what people want, e.g. kroner bills, and what people have kroner bills to sell. The case is similar to that of a dealer in commodities, who makes his living by knowing which people have his particular line of commodities to sell, and which people want to buy. He does the business cheaper than the banks could do it themselves with the same degree of efficiency. If a bank had its own official to buy bills he would have to be a high-salaried man with a wide knowledge of the bill market, he would have to have his clerks and typists, and he would have to employ the bank's capital. In the end, he would cost the bank more than does the commission or margin paid to the bill-broker. So well recognized is this fact, that bankers not only buy bills from the bill-brokers, but themselves finance the bill-brokers. The major part of a bill-broker's business is done on money borrowed from the banks against the deposit of bills or bonds as security; and the bill-brokers make their living by having in their portfolio bills of just the kind and just the maturity which they know the banks will want. On occasion the bill-broker works entirely on commission. In the ordinary way, his profits are mainly derived from the margin between bill and money rates,[1] i.e. between the rate of discount which he deducts from a bill when paying cash for it and the rate of interest which he has paid to the bank for the loan of that cash. In addition there is of course the interest on his capital, which is in the form of investments which can be pledged as security for the loans he requires.[2]

The price at which bills are sold is quoted in terms of the rate of discount that is deducted from them, and that rate is known as the market rate. This is the rate on which we have to fix our attention. It is only one of a number of rates of interest obtaining in the money market. These rates are more or less connected. Bank rate is one of them. Bank rate and market rate do not necessarily vary with one another; the exact relations between them we shall examine later on. Deposit rate is another, being the rate of interest allowable by the joint-stock and merchant banks on balances

[1] See lecture by D. Spring Rice on the money market printed in the "Banker's Magazine," issue of March, 1922.

[2] *Ibid.*

deposited with them subject to withdrawal at seven days' notice. Deposit rate varies in an upward or downward direction with bank rate. The rate of interest on loans to bill-brokers is generally, but not always, a fraction higher than deposit rate. The rate of interest charged by bill-brokers on bills, i.e. the market rate of discount, is necessarily a little higher than the rate of interest which bill-brokers pay on their loans from the banks.

The factors which determine the market rate of discount, i.e. the price of bills in terms of cash, are more complicated than those which determine the prices of commodities in terms of cash, for not only the supply of bills, but also the supply of cash at the disposal of the short loan market, is constantly fluctuating. The causes of the fluctuations in the supply of cash in the money market cannot be gone into here : obviously they will largely derive from the state of trade and of the investment market and from taxation.

So far as the fluctuations in the supplies of bills are concerned, we have first of all to distinguish between commercial bills and finance bills.[1] The fluctuations in supply mainly affect finance bills and only secondarily commercial bills. So far as the latter are concerned, it is evident that the price that has to be paid for financial accommodation in the money market will not immediately affect the supply of commercial bills that come forward for discounting, because these commercial bills will be simply the results of transactions entered into a considerable time ago, and entered into by merchants whose profits normally are large enough to enable them not to be vitally interested in marginal variations in the rate at which their bills will have to be discounted. A change in money market conditions will not in the first instance affect the supply of com-

[1] See Chapter IV.

mercial bills. The change may, as we shall see, affect that supply later on if it continues long enough. But the supply of finance bills is affected very much indeed by conditions in the money market. It is not difficult to see why bills of this kind are much more susceptible to money market influences. The mercantile drawer of a finance bill loses the discount on the bill when he discounts it, he loses the acceptance house's commission, and he loses the interest on the amount for the two days before maturity when he has to put the accepting house in funds. He has therefore to think carefully about the rate at which he can discount the bill before drawing, in order to see whether it is worth his while to pay for the additional accommodation. The less profit he is making on his business, the more carefully he will look at the amount the accommodation costs. It may happen that although these facilities are at his disposal, he refrains from using them, because a marginal increase in discount rates makes it just not worth his while. In other words, the drawing of such bills may depend entirely upon the marginal fluctuations in the market rate of discount. And if that is true of a mercantile drawer, it would be much more true of a merchant banker in Paris, Berlin, or Stockholm. A merchant banker does not work on a fairly substantial margin of profit, but on a much finer margin. He relies on being able to use the funds which he acquires at a profit only slightly greater than the cost: on being able to lend money at a slightly higher rate than that at which he borrows it. Whether a foreign banker in possession of a number of blank credits with London accepting houses uses them or not will quite definitely be determined by the market rate of discount. It will depend from time to time on the rates at which his London bankers will discount such drafts whether he draws or not. These are primarily the kind of bills we have in mind when we speak of the volume of bills expanding and contracting.

We are now in a position to examine in detail the effect of variations in the market rate of discount on exchange rates.[1] Assuming first a decline in market rate. (1) Other things being equal, a low market rate of discount evidently will encourage the foreigner who has facilities for drawing on accepting houses in London to use them. A merchant banker in Paris will, other things being equal, be encouraged by the fact that he can discount drafts cheaply, i.e. sell them in London for something near their face value, to bring them into existence, and that reasoning will apply more or less to the bulk of people abroad who have drawing facilities in London. Therefore a volume of sterling bills will be brought into existence which otherwise would not have been created. Sterling bills, being accordingly more numerous, will become cheaper, and the amount of foreign currency to be given for them less; in other words, the exchanges will tend to go against Britain. (2) Again, the various interest rates allowed by the joint-stock and merchant banks move together, and a low market rate of discount implies a low deposit rate. When, therefore, the merchant banker in Paris, by drawing as above, provided himself with funds in London, his inclination will be to withdraw them from London to another centre where rates of interest are higher and they can earn more. (3) The same will be true of a large quantity of the balances held in London at the disposal of foreigners. These balances will be remitted abroad by foreign currency drafts, so that a demand for such drafts will be set up.

A low market rate of discount therefore tends to increase the supply of sterling bills and to increase the

[1] On this subject, see Withers: "Money-Changing," Chapter VII.

demand for foreign currency, both of which factors tend to make the exchanges adverse to Britain.

In the case of a high market rate, the reasoning will be reversed. (1) The fact that bills in London cost a good deal to discount will tend to prevent foreigners drawing on London; the tendency will therefore be for the volume of sterling bills to get less, because as they run off they will not be renewed; and as the volume of sterling bills becomes less, the price will go up. That means the exchanges will tend to go in our favour. (2) Again, under the same conditions of a high market rate, foreigners who have sold goods to Britain and been paid in London, will tend to leave their money in London in order to earn the benefit of the high market rate of discount. If a foreign merchant who has sold us goods has no particular use for his money for two or three weeks, he can leave it on deposit with one of the London merchant banks in order to obtain the benefit of the high rates of interest obtaining in London. The tendency therefore will be for foreign creditors to leave their money here instead of having it sent to them; that means that the banks, instead of having to buy foreign currency drafts to remit to these foreign clients, will not have to do so. To that extent there will be less demand for foreign currency drafts, which again means that the value of sterling will go up. (3) Similarly, merchant bankers with balances abroad will send their money here in order to earn the high rates of interest in operation. These balances, it must be remembered, do not consist of investment money; they are floating balances, and they float towards high rates of interest. Once here they can be employed in discounting bills and obtaining the high rate of discount available, or put out on deposit with one of the London discount houses and earn the high deposit rates that will normally accompany a high market rate. The effect of (1) is to diminish the volume of sterling bills in existence; the effect of (2) is to diminish the demand for foreign currency; the effect of (3) is to set up a demand abroad for sterling drafts: francs, dollars, and marks are used to buy sterling drafts. In all these three ways the raising of the market rate of discounts operates to turn the exchanges in our favour.

The reactions so far described as the result of market rate being raised or lowered have all related to finance bills. It is this class of bills which are in the first instance affected by changes in market rate. But a long-continued low or high market rate also affects the supply of commercial bills. In the case of a long-continued low rate it tends to increase the supply of commercial bills; a long-continued high rate, to diminish it. In the case of the low rate, a buyer of commodities who requires accommodation can get it easily, for not only can he discount bills cheaply, but also a low market rate implies that other rates of interest are low too. In other words, the merchant will get his bank overdrafts cheaper. That state of easy accommodation continued over a long period will encourage importers. This means the coming into existence of a number of bills drawn on London by suppliers abroad, which would not have come into existence had it not been for the fact that imports were particularly easy to finance. A low market rate, therefore, over a period of time, will tend to increase the volume also of commercial bills, and thereby to turn the exchanges further against us.

To that statement there is an exception. If the long-continued supply of cheap money is due to the fact that there is very little business doing, because confidence has been shaken, perhaps by some big failure, or by political conditions, then it may be that the absence of business confidence will discourage buyers more than the cheap money will encourage them and the excess of commercial bills will not come into existence. Such is the condition of things at the time of writing.[1]

A long-continued high market rate makes accommodation dear and hence discourages buyers. Thereby it tends to diminish the volume of commercial bills coming into existence and hence to turn the exchanges in our favour.

This statement is also subject to an exception. If the dear money is due to widespread optimism, belief in the continuance of an existing boom and of a state of rising prices, then dear money may fail to deter buyers. Such was the case from about November, 1919, to April, 1920.

Having investigated the effect on exchange rates of variations on the market rate of discount, we are in a position to examine the manner in which another one of the interest rates, namely Bank Rate, was used as the regulator of the exchanges. In pre-war times it was possible, by raising bank rate, to turn adverse exchanges in our favour.

Let us take the case where the exchange was unfavourable. Owing to prolonged depression, the adverse exchange failed to stimulate the export trade and thus act as an automatic corrective, as it normally would do. High interest rates abroad attracted our gold, and the exchanges continued to go against us. The Paris rate, let us say, was down to 25·17, i.e. it was approaching the point (about 25·15) at which gold would begin to leave the country. It was under such conditions that the regulating machinery of the Bank of England's rate came into operation.

It may be asked: Why the Bank of England more than any other bank? Supposing gold was sent abroad by bullion dealers, in what way did that directly affect the Bank of England? In this way: the Bank of England keeps the only material gold reserve in the country, so that the sending of any quantity of gold

[1] July, 1922.

out of the country meant the diminution, sooner or later, of the reserve in the Bank of England's vaults. The bullion dealers might be acting for a banker, or for a foreign banker with an office in London. They would simply present notes at the Bank of England to the value of the gold they wanted, and the bank was bound by statute to give gold for those notes up to any amount. When, therefore, the exchange began to approach the lower gold point, the Bank of England was forced to take an active interest in the matter.

It will be remembered that we are assuming pre-war conditions, and that the most important of those conditions was that the currency of England was gold, or paper convertible into gold, and the possession of British currency was a claim to so much gold.

The ultimate aim of the Bank of England was to protect its gold reserve, and this required that the exchanges should be turned in our favour. This it aimed at accomplishing by raising the market rate of discount. The raising of that rate, once it could be accomplished, would affect the turning of adverse into favourable exchanges in the manner already explained. The Bank of England's immediate aim, then, was to raise the market rate of discount.

Its first step was to raise bank rate. The sequence of events in the money market was then, according to Mr. Withers,[1] as follows. The next step lay with the joint-stock banks. Everybody in Lombard Street knew that the aim of the Bank of England in raising its rate was to send up interest rates generally and the market rate of discount in particular. The joint-stock banks might either follow the lead or not. If they decided to follow the lead, they were accepting as a fact that money was going to become dearer, i.e. that cash would become more valuable as against bills. Their aim would then

[1] "The Meaning of Money," Chapter XII.

become to increase their cash in hand, and this they would do in three ways :

(*a*) They would raise their rate of interest on deposits.

(*b*) They would for the present refrain from buying any more bills.

(*c*) They would call in their loans at call and short notice.

Their short-dated loans would have been made in the main to bill-brokers. This calling in placed the bill-brokers in a very unfortunate position. They were hit in three ways :

(1) First of all the bills they had in their portfolio became automatically less in value, since interest rates went up. Interest rates going up meant that more discount would be deducted from the bills when the holders wanted to turn them into cash than had been the case before. A bill was worth less in terms of cash, so that the whole portfolio of bills which the broker was carrying became worth less.

(2) The banks were calling in the loans on which the bill brokers had been financing their business.

(3) The banks were not buying bills to the extent that they had been, just when the brokers wanted to turn them into cash.

Obviously, the bill-broker had to get financial accommodation somewhere, and, the joint-stock banks refusing to help him, the only place he could get it was at the Bank of England. The Bank of England was perfectly willing to let him have it, but on its own terms : approved bills it would discount at bank rate, loans it would make at a half per cent. above bank rate. That meant that bank rate had become the effective market rate. People who had bills to discount had to discount them at bank rate. Bank rate determined the price for advances. Rates of interest had been raised all round ; the market rate of discount had been forced up to the level of bank rate. The Bank of England had achieved its object. The raising of market rate had the effect of turning the exchanges in our favour in the manner described in the last chapter.

Now let us suppose the joint-stock banks had not followed the lead of the Bank of England. The Bank of England wanted to make money dearer, but the joint-stock banks did not follow its lead. They neither refrained from buying bills nor called in their short loans to the bill-brokers. The Bank of England could make them follow its lead. It could go into the money market and borrow money, which it did not need, in order to make money scarcer. Money became scarce as a result of the Bank's borrowings. Everybody in Lombard Street knew that, whether they liked it or not, money was becoming dearer. From that point, the developments were exactly as in the previous case. The joint-stock banks had no option but to refrain from buying bills, and strengthen their cash reserves by calling in their short loans and raising deposit rates. The bill-brokers had to borrow. Once again, therefore, the bank rate became effective, and the forces described in the last chapter were set in motion and turned the exchanges in our favour.

To readers who have seen bank rate raised and the dollar exchange remain unfavourable,[1] this reasoning may seem somewhat abstract, but in practice in pre-war times it was very real indeed. A good illustration of the reality of it occurred in 1907, on the occasion of a financial panic in New York. The Bank of England raised its rate and thereby attracted remittances from all over the world, which enabled it to supply New York with the means to tide over the crisis. The best illustration of the effectiveness of a rise in bank rate in turning the exchanges in our favour, however, occurred in the last days of July

[1] December, 1919, and April, 1920.

and the first days of August, 1914. With the approach of war, every one in all the principal cities of the world who had claims elsewhere tried to realize them in terms of his own currency. All the financial centres of the world were trying to bring their balances home. The Bank of England raised its rate from 4 per cent. to 10 per cent. in the course of a few days, and this was so effective that the exchanges went violently in favour of this country and remittances arrived from almost every foreign centre until the means of remittance were exhausted.

The reason why the machinery does not work to-day as it did before August, 1914, is that war finance has altered entirely the conditions obtaining in the money market—how, we shall understand after we have dealt with the matter of paper money and inflation. But it is possible to say here that the result of that alteration has been to destroy the two assumptions, on which the reasoning of this chapter has been based. The first of those assumptions was that English currency was convertible into gold; the second was that claims which London had on various financial centres could be realized in gold if necessary. Those assumptions were both true before the war, and neither is true to-day. The first is not true because there is a legal prohibition on the export of gold, and gold is at a premium as compared with the paper pound. The second assumption falls because in all other financial centres, except New York, the export of gold is prohibited, and Berlin, Paris, Frankfort, and Rome have not the gold to send to discharge their liabilities to us.

CHAPTER XI

INFLATION

Inflation of currency and inflation of credit—Relation between the two—How both were brought about by war-finance—Ways and Means Advances—Effect of inflation on prices and exchange rates—Quantity Theory of Money.

WE now come on to the last and most interesting section of the whole subject—to the consideration, namely, of the sixth factor which causes exchange fluctuations, i.e. the depreciation of currency by the issue of paper money. Of all the disastrous effects of the war on finance and the foreign exchanges, that of the over-issue of paper money is the most fundamental. This over-issue is bound up with what is known as "inflation," and it is necessary to be clear as to what is meant by that term. There are two things which may be inflated, credit and currency. Inflation of currency means an increase in the volume of currency without an equivalent increase in its gold backing or in the volume of other commodities represented by it. Inflation of credit means an increase in the volume of credit without any equivalent increase in either the gold basis or in the volume of commodities available. The relations between the inflation of currency and the inflation of credit have been the subject of a great deal of technical discussion by specialists. In actual fact, the two have always during the war period appeared together, like the high temperature and the congestion of the lungs in Spanish influenza; and the effect of the combination has been the depreciation of the currencies affected, i.e. their diminution in value in terms of gold and in terms of other currencies not so affected.

On the whole it seems best to regard the inflation of currency as the effect of the inflation of credit, the latter coming first in the order of cause and effect. Our problem is, then, twofold: (*a*) How did the inflation of credit arise, and how did that necessitate an inflation of currency? and (*b*) given an inflation of currency, how does that depreciate the currency?

The inflation of credit we have described as the increase in the volume of credit, i.e. purchasing power, in existence without a corresponding increase in the volume of commodities on which the credit is based. The inflation of credit arose directly out of one of the methods of financing the war, and was adopted both in this and other countries. It was one of the results of the war finance.

There are three ways, and three ways only, in which a war can be financed: taxation, borrowing, and inflation.[1] Taxation consists in the taking of purchasing power by the Government from private individuals. As a result of taxation the purchasing power of the individual is restricted to exactly the same extent as the purchasing power of the Government is increased. For every 5s. which the Government takes from us in income tax, we have 5s. less to spend. There is no inflation there, as there is no increase in the purchasing power. The second method of financing a war is borrowing: borrowing money which has been saved. When some of our more fortunate citizens, whose duties confined them to the home front during the war, subscribed for War Loan out of their savings, they diminished their potential purchasing power by exactly the same extent as that

[1] See Withers: "War-Time Financial Problems," Chapter III.

to which the Government's purchasing power was increased by the transfer of the money for War Loan to the Government's credit. There is no inflation there, because once again there is no increase in purchasing power. The fact that there is no inflation in either of these cases does not of course mean that they are without injurious effect on the national welfare. In so far as the money taken from the taxpayer, or subscribed by the applicant for War Loan, would have been spent on personal luxury, no harm is done. The wealth is wasted, alike whether it is spent on munitions or in luxurious living. But it might have been spent in a manner which would have ultimately increased the production of wealth. If, for example, instead of investing £100 in War Loan, "A" had invested it in a cotton mill, the result of his expenditure would have been ultimately to increase the production of yarn or of piece-goods. As it was, the £100 he subscribed to War Loan was spent by the Government in munitions, which were destroyed without producing any wealth. To the extent to which the money confiscated by taxation or subscribed to loans would otherwise have been applied to wealth production, to that extent such war finance is harmful. Our point here, however, is simply that in these cases there is no immediate increase in purchasing power relative to commodities, and consequently no immediate rise in prices.

The third method of financing the war, by inflation itself, is also operated by borrowing on the part of the Government, but by borrowing of a different kind. Inflation of credit in this country has taken place through the borrowing by the Government of purchasing power which did not exist. This apparently fantastic procedure took two different forms. The forms were different according as the Government borrowed the purchasing power which did not exist from the joint-stock banks, or from the Bank of England.[1]

(*a*) *Borrowing from the Joint-Stock Banks.*—Considerable pressure was put by the Government on the banks to induce them to subscribe for War Loan and to create credits which should be used to facilitate subscriptions from the banks' clients for War Loan. The banks accordingly drew on their balances at the Bank of England either to themselves subscribe for War Loan, or to create in their books credits out of which they could render to their clients the necessary overdrafts to enable those clients to subscribe. Government securities were issued to the banks and their clients, in exchange for which the Government received the purchasing power represented by the banks' former balances with the Bank of England. So far, there was no inflation, because the increased spending power which the Government now had was compensated for by the decrease in the banks' balances at the Bank of England. The Government used the spending power thus put into its hands to pay contractors. The contractors paid in the drafts they received from the Government Departments to their own banking accounts. That increased the general volume of deposits which the joint-stock banks held. Out of that increased volume of deposits the joint-stock banks were able to replenish their balances at the Bank of England, which had been depleted in the first instance. The position then was that the banks' balances at the Bank of England were as they were before: the contractors' balances at their own banks were larger than they were before by exactly the amount of the increased spending power which had been created. In other words, the amount of credit available, that is, the amount

[1] See, on the three following paragraphs, Mr. McKenna's speech at the annual meeting of the London Joint City and Midland Bank in 1920, reported in the weekly press under date, January 31, 1920.

of purchasing power available, had been increased by the extent to which the War Loan had been paid for out of credit created for the purpose, such credit created for the purpose being represented among the banks and their clients by Government securities. There had been an increase in the total volume of purchasing power, against which there was no increase whatever in the total volume of commodities in existence. That, in the terms of our definition, constitutes inflation. This was the first way in which inflation occurred.

(*b*) *Borrowing from the Bank of England.*—The second way is worse. It consisted of borrowing by the Government from the Bank of England on Ways and Means advances. The procedure in this case was that the Bank of England, instead of the joint-stock banks, created an overdraft in favour of the Government, which drew on it to pay contractors. The contractors paid the drafts into their accounts at the banks, which as before increased the total volume of banking deposits. This enabled the joint-stock banks to increase their balances at the Bank of England. The difference from the previous method consisted in this: that in the second case the joint-stock banks' balances had not been depleted at the commencement of the operation.

In this case, therefore, at the conclusion of the whole operation the position was that there had been an increase (*i*) in the total volume of the joint-stock banks' balances at the Bank of England, and (*ii*) in the total volume of bank deposits. Now the joint-stock banks' balances at the Bank of England constitute the funds on the basis of which the joint-stock banks found their advances to customers. Therefore, when their balances with the Bank of England were increased, the banks were in a position to make more advances than they had made before, so that in this case the inflation which finally resulted from the borrowing by the Government from the Bank of England was two-fold. There was an increase in the volume of banking deposits to the credit of the general public, and secondly there was an increase in the credit facilities which the joint-stock banks were able to grant. In other words, the dose of inflation under this second procedure was a double one, and not as in the first case a single dose. In both cases the result was to create an increase in the total volume of purchasing power available with no corresponding increase in the production of commodities.

We are now able to understand why the inflation of credit, as described above, brought in its trail an inflation of the currency. Many of the cheques which the contractors drew on their balances with the banks had to be paid in the form of £1 notes, because the money was required for paying wages. The banks therefore required an additional stock of Bradburys. They got them by drawing on their balances at the Bank of England. A certain amount, corresponding of course to the quantity of Bradburys they required, was transferred in the books of the Bank of England from the credit of the bank in question to the credit of the currency note account, and the Bradburys were then issued to the banks. Such was the actual procedure whereby the currency note was put into circulation. The issue of paper money is seen to be an adjunct to the inflation of credit, but an indispensable adjunct in the sense that only by that means could the additional purchasing power created be made effective. The volume of currency had been increased without any corresponding increase in the volume of commodities. But it is well to remember that, as Mr. McKenna has put it, "currency notes are not so much the effective cause of the rise in prices, but rather the rain-gauge that measures the quantity of rain." The whole of this question of inflation of credit and inflation of currency can best be studied in detail in two documents. The first is the Cunliffe Committee Report issued in 1919, and obtainable at H.M. Stationery Office, and the second is the report of Mr. McKenna's speech at the annual meeting of the London Joint City and Midland Bank in 1920.[1]

Having seen how war finance brought about the inflation of credit, and how that in turn caused inflation of currency, we proceed to the second of the two questions we asked at the beginning of this chapter: the effect of the inflation of the currency on the exchanges.

That effect is merely part of the general effect of the inflation of the currency on its value. The value of a currency can be expressed in two ways: in prices, which represent its exchange value at home; and in exchange rates, which represent its value abroad. The general effect of the inflation of the currency was to bring about a decline in its value. That decline was expressed in (*a*) a rise in prices, i.e. the necessity to give more currency in exchange for given commodities; and (*b*) a decline in its foreign exchange value in terms of the dollar, i.e. a decline in the number of dollars which had to be given up for one pound. The reason why other foreign exchange rates have not shown the same features is that other foreign currencies have been subject to the same influences as our own, many of them to a much greater degree.

The relation between the volume of currency and its value is given by what is known as the "Quantity Theory of Money." The quantity theory of money is in effect this: given that at a certain time there exists a certain volume of commodities and a certain volume of

[1] There is also a useful article in the "Times Trade Supplement" of May 28, 1921, by Frank Morrison, headed "Inflation," and a detailed study of the whole subject in Prof. Pigou's "The Political Economy of War."

money, there will be an equation between the two representing the number of units of money that have to be given for a certain unit of commodity value. If, while the volume of commodities remains unchanged, the volume of money increases, then the number of units of money that will have to be given in exchange for the same unit of commodity value will also increase. That is the quantity theory of money. As expressed, it would be accepted as correct by economists generally. Criticisms are sometimes directed against the theory, but on examination it will be found that they do not affect the theory as stated above. One line of criticism, for example, depends upon the meaning of the word "money." Money, in the sense we are using it,[1] is not the same as currency: we take money in the general sense of purchasing power. Another line of criticism can be directed against the quantity theory of money if it is stated in the form set out some time ago in a financial journal: "If with a given quantity of money and a given quantity of goods the price of the latter be 100, then with an increase of 50 per cent. in the quantity of money, the price of the goods will be advanced in a like ratio, or if the operation be reversed, the percentage will fall in a like ratio." It is by no means certain that where there is an increase in the volume of money and no equivalent increase in the volume of goods, prices will rise in the same ratio. The ratio between the increase in prices and the increase in the volume of currency depends upon the way in which inflation has occurred and on the velocity of circulation of the currency, i.e. the rate at which currency units pass from hand to hand. What is certain is that an increase in the volume of currency causes an increase in the general price level. The number of units of currency which have to be given up in exchange for a given block of commodities

[1] See Chapter I.

increases, i.e. the value of the currency unit declines. The increase in the supply of these units has brought about a decline in their value. This decline in value will be expressed, not only in terms of commodity prices, but also in terms of foreign exchange rates, unless the same causes which have caused a decline in the value of the currency here have been operative at the same time elsewhere to the same or to a greater extent.

Such was the process according to the quantity theory of money, which is not merely a theory but a description of what has actually happened in this and other countries during the war, and in other countries since. It can be, and has been, proved dozens of times by various sets of figures.

(1) In the spring of 1920, the Belgian Minister of Finance, in reviewing the financial position of that country, remarked on the fact that although (he was comparing the Belgian trade balances of January and February) in January Belgian exports only just balanced their imports, while in February exports were 65,000,000 francs as against 44,000,000 francs in January, still the exchange had continued to go against Belgium. From that he drew the conclusion that the country's exchange position was not entirely dependent upon its balance of trade. The explanation why a favourable trade balance had been accompanied by a decline in the rate of exchange was that during this period Belgium had continued to increase her uncovered note circulation.

(2) There is an official publication by the Government of this country, Command Paper 434 of 1920, table 3 of which compares the expansion of the eleven principal countries' currencies with their rates of exchange on London. The table shows that the average expansion of the currencies as compared to the United Kingdom, which is taken as 100, is 133·5, while the average rate of exchange per cent. of parity of those countries on London

is 134·1. In other words, the decline in those countries' rates of exchange practically coincides with the expansion of their paper currency.[1] Similarly, statistics relating to the note issue of the countries engaged in the war follow, very broadly speaking, the same curve as is described by price curves. It will be remembered that the great rise in prices in this country took place during the last two years of the war, and the greatest expansion of the Treasury note circulation took place also during this same period. It was in the summer of 1916 that the over-issue of paper money began to assume large proportions, and it was following that time that the rise in prices ceased to be an ordinary rise, and became a series of jumps. The same connexion between inflation and the rise in prices was observed in Germany. There is in fact a considerable parallelism between the financial history of this country and of Germany during the war. Taxation, indeed, played a much greater part in Britain than it could possibly do in Germany, by reason, in the latter case, of the limited powers of the Federal Government in regard to direct taxation, the falling-off of indirect taxation owing to the blockade, and the smaller volume of accumulated liquid resources. But in both cases there was the supersession of the customary foreign exchange operations by credits arranged, in the case of Germany, with the European neutrals. In both cases, moreover, the great volume of war-time inflation occurred after the close of 1916. In 1918–1919 the German Revolution and the Peace conditions differentiated the two processes by creating political conditions which rendered possible the stopping of inflation in this country while partly favouring and partly necessitating its continuance in Germany.

It is clear that inflation of credit, accompanied by the

[1] The point was made by Mr. H. H. O'Farrell in the " Sunday Times " of April 6, 1920.

increase of inconvertible paper currency, leads to a depreciation of exchange values in terms of currencies not subject to the same degree of inflation.

We have next to examine how far the decline in a currencies exchange value, due to inflation, is likely to go.

CHAPTER XII

PURCHASING POWER PARITY

Different methods of increasing volume of currency—Convertible and inconvertible paper—Gold shipments and world prices—Purchasing power and exchange value—Purchasing power parity—Price levels and exchange rates—Limitations of the theory of purchasing power parity.

IT will have been observed that in speaking of the depreciation of the exchanges due to inflation we have been careful to speak of the increase of "inconvertible" paper currency. In dealing with the effects on the exchanges of an increase in the volume of currency it is necessary to distinction between an increase due on one hand to putting into circulation additional gold or paper convertible into gold, and an increase due on the other hand to the issue of inconvertible paper. It is true that in both cases the quantity theory applies and prices rise. But in the first case the exchanges are not affected, while in the second they are. This distinction and the reason for it are vital to the elucidation of the problem how far a decline in exchange values due to inflation is likely to go.

From 1896 to 1914 the volume of gold in existence was increased by reason of the exploitation of the Rand Mines, and owing to that increase in the volume of gold, and of the credit based on it, prices rose steadily during this period. But the exchange value of our currency did not decline. The war-time increases in the volume of currency, on the other hand, consisted of inconvertible paper: and not only did prices rise, but exchange values declined.

It is true that Treasury notes are theoretically convertible into gold. But not only are difficulties put in the way of people who want gold for notes, but the export of gold has been prohibited as a punishable offence. People have in fact been sent to prison for doing what was a normal part of a bullion dealer's business before the war. If therefore the holder of a Treasury note succeeds in getting a sovereign for his Bradbury he can do nothing with it. The convertibility of the note has in fact been destroyed.

The difference between an increase of paper convertible into gold and an increase of inconvertible paper is not merely one of degree. It is true that in the case of gold, or of a paper currency freely convertible into gold, a sudden increase in the volume of currency cannot obtain, as it is not possible to increase suddenly the volume of gold available for circulation. This fact ensures the relative stability of a currency freely convertible into gold, as were the currencies of the principal European countries previous to the war. In so far, however, during the pre-war period, as the volume of gold in circulation and of the credit based upon it increased more rapidly than the volume of commodities, prices rose, but without any corresponding decline in exchange values.

The essential difference between the two ways of increasing the volume of currency lies in this, that where the increase is due to putting additional gold into circulation, the increase in prices will be world-wide. A portion of the additional gold will be drawn away to other countries and will affect their currencies in terms of commodity values to an equal extent, so that the exchange values of the various currencies will remain the same. From 1896 to 1914 the gold point theory was in operation: gold could be, and when necessary was, shipped abroad and operated to equalize the rise in prices in the various countries. This it did in two ways: (*a*) The mere fact of the import of gold tended to raise prices, both by directly increasing the volume of potential circulating media and by enabling credit to be created on that basis, while the export of it exerted the opposite effect in tending to reduce prices in the country of export. (*b*) Because gold was itself a commodity, an export from the country with the higher price level and an import to the country with the lower price level, the fact of its shipment *pro tanto* altered the balance of indebtedness in favour of the exporting country, and thus tended to turn the exchanges in its favour. In this way it happened that although in England from 1896 to 1914 the value of money in terms of goods went down, yet the exchange value of our money did not go down, because the value of other countries' money in terms of their goods was going down in about the same ratio as ours. The equation between the pound on one hand, and the franc, mark, and dollar on the other, remained the same. The value of these units in terms of gold remained constant. The whole process furnished an instructive example of the way in which gold served as an international currency.[1]

In the case of an increase in the volume of inconvertible paper currency, no such general effect is produced. Prices are raised only in the country which issues the additional paper. Inconvertible paper currency has no intrisinc value. Its value is its value as a token: what the people of a country have agreed to accept it as being worth. Its foreign exchange value depends upon its purchasing power in the country of origin; as this declines, so does its exchange value. That value cannot be restored by shipping gold abroad, for such shipments are prohibited. The extent to which the decline will

[1] See T. E. Gregory: "The Foreign Exchanges before, during, and after the War."

go is a matter which would appear not to be susceptible of exact determination. During the war, the exchanges were kept in a state of suspended animation. Since the war, the principal example of a depreciated currency, the mark, has been rendered invalid for the purposes of this reasoning by the fact that its movements have been mainly dependent on political factors and on reparation payments. In the case of every currency, many factors other than inflation have been at work on the exchanges, just as they have on prices. But it seems safe to say that inflation will depreciate the exchange value of a currency to at least the extent to which it raises prices.[1] Its influence on exchange value may be greater than on prices, since the element of apprehension, of discounting an unfavourable future, plays a larger part in exchange transactions conducted with or between foreigners than it does in determining commodity prices at home. The exchange value, in other words, will depend not only on its actual purchasing power but on its potential purchasing power, that is to say, the purchasing power which exchange dealers believe it will have in the near future. Its value is the measure of the goods that it is expected to be able to buy. Where a country is not producing any goods, the value goes down to nil, as it has done in Russia. The activities of speculators in the currencies of the various European countries simply amounts to the discounting beforehand of the probabilities in regard to the purchasing power of the paper currencies. The continued increase of paper money thus produces on exchange rates certainly the same effects as it does on home prices; and may have another, secondary, effect in lowering the credit of the issuing country.

The first statement generalizes what has occurred, as a result of the war, to the currencies of the European

[1] See article by Prof. J. M. Keynes in "Manchester Guardian" Commercial Reconstruction Number I.

countries as compared with that of the United States. Its truth is best illustrated by measuring the depreciation of the gold sovereign in terms of the paper pound, which will be found to be also the measure of the depreciation of the Anglo-American Exchange. Before the war the price of gold was fixed, as the Mint would always buy it at 85s. per oz. of fine gold. English standard gold was $\frac{11}{12}$th fine, and was therefore accordingly bought at 77s. 10½d. per oz. On a given day in 1922 the price of gold was 95s. per oz. The price therefore of one ounce of standard gold, i.e. of 480 grains, was $\frac{11}{12} \times 95$. In a gold sovereign there are 123·2 grains of gold. Therefore the price of the gold in a gold sovereign in terms of our present-day currency was:

$$\frac{11 \times 95 \times 123{\cdot}2}{12 \times 480} = 22{\cdot}37\text{s.},$$

i.e. the paper pound had depreciated 2·37s. on every 22·37s. or nearly 10·6 per cent. On the same day the dollar was quoted at 4·36, i.e. a depreciation, when comparison is made with par value, of ·51 for every 4·87, or nearly 10·5 per cent. Similarly, about a year ago, when the dollar rate was 3·88, the price of fine gold was £5 6s. 8d. per oz., so that the depreciation at that time was in each case about 20 per cent.

A comparison [1] again, of the prices in Italian paper lire of (*a*) the pound sterling and (*b*) 100 gold lire, made in March, 1920, when the pound sterling was relatively stable, showed that the two sets of prices were following the same curve. The figures showed that the depreciation of the paper lire, measured in terms of (*a*) the gold lire and of (*b*) the stable pound sterling, was roughly the same in both cases.

It is this inflation, which, more than anything else,

[1] The Tables are given in "Anglo-Italian Review" of March, 1920.

is the cause of the present situation of the European exchanges. This country, although it has changed its currency from gold to one of inconvertible paper, has nevertheless over-issued paper money less than any other important gold-currency country in the world except the United States. The result is that on the one hand this country's currency in terms of the dollar has declined in value, and on the other hand that in terms of other countries' currencies it has appreciated, not because it itself has increased its intrinsic value, but because the other countries have over-issued paper money to a greater extent. The League of Nations published some very interesting economic memoranda in 1920, showing that at that time the principal countries of the world, exclusive of Russia, had increased their note-circulation eight times over. That conveys an idea of the extent to which inconvertible paper money had taken the place of gold as the basis of the principal currencies of the world. Since then, the output of inconvertible paper has increased.

The element of theoretical reasoning which surrounds the exact relations between inflation, the exchanges, and prices must not be allowed to obscure the fact, which is as well established as anything in economics can be, that inflation causes enormous rises in prices and declines in exchange values.

It follows that the exchange fluctuations of inflated currencies present quite a different problem from those of pre-war days. They can no longer be correlated to Mint Par, which assumes convertibility into gold. Our post-war experience is so varied that it is difficult to generalize from it. It seems that the present-day exchanges tend to move about a new par called " Purchasing Power Parity."[1] The old Mint Par was obtained by

[1] The following explanation of purchasing power parity is based on the article by Prof. J. M. Keynes previously cited.

comparing the amounts of gold which two standard coins represented. The new purchasing power parity is obtained by comparing prices in the two countries in question. We find that a certain block of commodities can, after making certain allowances, be purchased in England for so many pounds and in Germany for so many marks. The division of that number of marks by the corresponding number of pounds gives as quotient a figure which represents the number of marks which a pound is worth in terms of purchasing power. Purchasing power parity, in other words, gives the exchange value of one currency in terms of another by means of an equation based on the prices obtaining in the two countries in question for certain kinds of goods. Mint Par was a comparison of quantities of gold; purchasing power parity is a comparison of certain kinds of commodity prices.

So far everything is straightforward enough; the difficulties occur in determining the two price levels to be compared. It will have been observed that in describing these price levels we made use of two qualifications. The price levels in question (*a*) were those of "certain kinds of goods"; and (*b*) these prices were to be compared "after making certain allowances."

As regards (*a*), the price levels compared are not the general price levels of the two countries, but the price levels in those countries of the goods entering into international trade. Goods and services produced at home for domestic consumption do not in either case enter into the calculation. The prices of, e.g., houses are excluded; so also are rail freights. The reason for this qualification is that a person, e.g. outside Germany, holding marks can only exercise the purchasing power of his marks on goods which it is legally and practically possible to import from Germany, i.e. on some portion of the goods entering into international trade.

As regards (*b*), in calculating the price level of the goods entering into international trade, allowance has to be made for freights, customs duties, and import and export prohibitions and regulations, for whether such prohibitions and regulations are made by governments or by organizations of producers or sellers, they may create artificial differences between home and export prices.

The price levels from the comparison of which the purchasing power parity between two ocuntries is obtaincd are thus differentiated from the general price levels obtaining in those countries, (*a*) by being restricted to the goods entering into international trade, and (*b*) by being subject to the adjustment described above. The equation between the two price levels so determined gives a new parity, round about which actual rates will fluctuate, as in pre-war days they fluctuated round Mint Par.

Why must this new equilibrium be established? Why must the exchange values of a currency approximate, sooner or later, to purchasing power parity?

Suppose exchange values are lower—e.g. suppose the Berlin exchange rate to be Mk. 2,200 = £1 and the purchasing power parity to be Mk. 2,000 = £1. The latter equation means that the price of a certain quantity of goods, after making the necessary allowances for freights and duties, etc., is £1 or Mk. 2,000. Now the cost of Mk. 2,000 is $£\frac{2,000}{2,200} = 18{\cdot}182$ shillings. The holder of sterling, accordingly, can by expending 18·182 shillings buy Mk. 2,000, which will purchase a quantity of goods which he can sell for £1, thereby making an exchange profit—in addition to whatever trading profit he may make—of 1·812 shillings on every pound. In such circumstances a demand will be set up for marks, and this demand, providing no other factors intervene, will send up their value. The demand will continue so long as the exchange value is less than purchasing power parity. On the other hand, suppose the exchange value of the currency to be higher than its purchasing power parity. In that case holders of the currency will exchange it for other currencies which command greater quantities of goods than do their own ; and this selling will diminish exchange value. The reasoning is the same as in the previous case applied in the reverse direction. The selling pressure will continue until the exchange value of the currency in question has declined to a point where the amount of the foreign currency exchanged for it will purchase only the same quantity of goods as are purchasable by itself, i.e. until purchasing power parity is reached.

This reasoning will incidentally have illustrated why, in calculating purchasing power parity, it is necessary to take the price levels of the goods entering into international trade, and to make the allowances set out under (*b*) above.

It will further be noted that these processes are what will take place provided no other factors intervene. It may happen on occasion that the exchange rate between two countries, as actually quoted, does not in fact approximate to purchasing power parity. In that case it is certain that there will be alterations in either the price levels in question—in one or both—or in the exchange rate, or in both ; and that as a result purchasing power parity and the exchange rate will approximately coincide. It may be that at the minute the exchange value of one of the currencies is depressed by political apprehensions ; these turn out to be ill-founded, and exchange values will then rise, for the reasons described above, until rates correspond with purchasing power parity. In this case it has been the exchange rate which has adjusted itself to the price level. On the other hand, political events, reparations payments or war-debt repayments may cause the exchange values of the currency affected permanently to decline. Once again there will be a gap between exchange rates and purchasing power parity. On this occasion the tendency for the exchange rate to improve in the manner described above is overborne by the effect of the blow dealt at the country's credit, wealth, or productive capacity. As therefore the decline in exchange values is permanent, imports will cost more and prices rise. The prices of the goods entering into international trade will rise until they reach the cost of replacement under the new conditions, i.e. until they reach world-prices. In this way a new purchasing power parity is reached which corresponds with exchange rates. In this sequence of events, which has happened more than once since the war in Germany, it is the price level which has adjusted itself to the exchange rate. Finally, it is conceivable that at a given moment the exchange rate, having suffered a permanent decline by reason of political events, might be temporarily depressed still further by apprehension which ultimately turns out to be ill-founded, while the price level had not yet felt the full force of the permanent decline. In this event the price level would still be rising while the exchange rate was recovering. The exchange rate and purchasing power parity would then be moving towards one another. This process would continue, for the reasons described above, until they approximately coincided. In this case both the price level and the exchange rate have adjusted themselves the one to the other.

Such, in very broad outline, is the doctrine of purchasing power parity. Its practical utility evidently is restricted by the necessity of limiting the price levels taken into consideration to those of the goods which enter into international trade. Attempts to correlate the general price levels with exchange rates assume that the general price level in a country rises and falls in the same manner as the prices of the goods entering into international trade. This assumption may only be true, at any given moment of time, to a limited and uncertain extent, as the divergence between the internal and the external value of the mark between 1920 and 1922 fully illustrates.[1] To calculate, in any given case, how far the general price level is subject to influences which are not operative on the prices of the goods which enter into international trade is evidently an extremely difficult matter. The theory of purchasing power parity cannot accordingly be applied to the general price level as determined by e.g. the Board of Trade Index Number of wholesale prices or the Labour Ministry's Index Number of retail prices. The practical utility of the theory is thus limited, but it nevertheless provides a useful general guide to the post-war movements of the exchanges.

Purchasing power parity, unlike mint par, is a variable figure: it varies with price levels. Before the war, price levels were limited in their movements by the same factor which limited the movements of exchange rates: the possibility of shipping gold. Prices expressed in terms of national currencies were in reality gold prices, for these currencies represented a claim to gold which could be enforced. Alterations in prices were accordingly alterations in gold prices. Such alterations were both gradual, since the supply of gold cannot suddenly be increased, and common to all gold-using countries, by reason of the possibility of shipping gold. An increase in prices in any one centre would mean the export of gold to other centres where prices were lower, i.e. where gold would purchase more; and the lessening of the

[1] In June, 1922, when general prices in Germany were very low when translated into sterling, the price of a suit of clothes was higher than the corresponding price in England.

supply of gold in the first centre reduced the credit based on it and caused prices there to fall again. The extent to which the relation of price levels to each other could alter was fixed therefore by the Gold Points. To-day, the possibility of shipping gold no longer remains. The countries with currencies of low value do not possess sufficient to ship, about half the world's available supply being already in the U.S.A. Currencies have lost their gold value, and prices and hence purchasing power parities depend on a number of variable factors such as the extent of industrial and agricultural production and the quantity of paper money a government prints. Many purchasing power parities have accordingly been separated from the Gold Points for an indefinite period. The only question now is whether they—and the exchange rates which tend to fluctuate about them—can be stabilized so as to avoid the tremendous fluctuations of recent years. But the issue of stabilizing rates is best left until we have considered in detail the causes and course of post-war fluctuations.

CHAPTER XIII

THE MARK

Decline up to Sept., 1921—Blockade—Peace terms—Costs of Army of Occupation—Revolutionary outbreaks—Decline up to August, 1922—Reparations—Coal deliveries—Upper Silesia—Failure of loan negotiations—Threats of French aggression—Increase in note circulation frequently effect, as well as cause, of decline in value of mark—Illusory nature of German export boom—Unfavourable trade balance—Effect of Reparations policy.

THE effects on the exchanges of the outbreak of the war in 1914 have already been briefly referred to; [1] and also the war-time expedients for pegging the Anglo-American rate. [2] During the war, all the exchanges remained in a state of suspended animation by reason of the control exercised in the belligerent countries over payments abroad. No doubt the artificial equilibrium thus maintained assisted considerably in obscuring the extent to which the economic basis of European civilization was being shattered.

In 1919 the exchanges were generally decontrolled, and the course followed since the artificial equilibrium of the war-years ended has registered the effects of the war and the resulting terms of peace on the economic health of the countries concerned. Certain of the more important of the movements and their significance will be considered in the next chapter. Here it is intended to examine the

[1] Chapter X. For a full account, see Withers: "The War and Lombard Street."

[2] Chapter VIII.

course of the German mark up to August, 1922, at which time it had become evident that this currency was following in the wake of the Polish mark and the Austrian krone. The case of the mark is worthy of especial attention by reason of the fact that before the war Germany was the greatest industrial Power on the Continent and that the devaluation of the mark (*die Entwertung der Mark*) has profoundly affected the welfare of this country both directly and indirectly, bearing as it does a share of responsibility for the unemployment existing here.

From about 80 after the signature of the Peace Treaty, the mark went up to 180 by December, 1919. In the spring of 1920 it declined further to about 270, recovered in the summer to about 135, and then fell away again fairly steadily to between 350 and 400 in September, 1921. The causes of this decline up to September, 1921, may be outlined as follows:

(1) The war left Germany terribly weakened. The disastrous effects of the blockade have not been fully realized outside Central and Eastern Europe. Unable to import on any large scale, the war was conducted mainly out of Germany's own resources. When the Armistice and the Revolution came, Germany was drained of all kinds of goods. Food and raw materials had to be imported; also a large quantity of manufactured goods which she herself could not produce until her people had recovered a little from semi-starvation, her factories restarted and her transport repaired.

(2) The Peace Treaty took away large and rich territories, such as the Saar coalfields, the Lorraine iron and the Alsace potash deposits, as well as the corn and potato-producing lands of Posen and West Prussia. Further, large deliveries of coal have continuously to be made by Germany to France, and also to Belgium and Italy. A large number of cows had also to be surrendered to France. The result of all this was that materials

which before were exported had now to be imported; food formerly produced at home had to be bought abroad.

(3) The Peace Treaty also took away the mercantile fleet, so that freights had to be paid in foreign currency.

(4) The Peace Treaty further hampered German exports by destroying German trading connexions.

(5) A large army of occupation and numerous expensive Allied commissions were quartered on Germany, while she also had to compensate her own nationals whose property overseas had been seized by the Allied Powers.

(6) The revolutionary outbreaks dissipated still further Germany's slender resources. Nor have the revolutionary Governments been immune from the extravagance in officialdom and the subsidizing of favoured classes of the population, which has been one of the universal consequences of the war.

The cumulative effects of these factors were (*a*) to necessitate large purchases of foreign currency, and (*b*) to render the German Government unable to meet its obligations save by the printing of paper money. The more paper money was printed, the more the mark declined in value abroad and at home; the more the value declined, the more marks were required to purchase foreign currencies or home manufactures and labour, and the higher, therefore, became the Government's expenditure; whereupon more marks were printed. The mark, in the grip of the jagged teeth of the vicious circle, continued to decline, but, taken over a period, in a more or less steady fashion until the autumn of 1921. Then its movements became as follows:

1921.—November 30th	- -	940–1,050
December 1st	- -	700– 805
,, 31st	- -	768– 774
1922.—January 31st	- -	855– 864
February 28th	- -	990–1,017

1922 (*con.*)	March 31st	1,250–1,380
	April 29th	1,250–1,260
	May 31st	1,219–1,240
	June 22nd	1,435–1,475
	,, 24th	1,485–1,506
	,, 26th	1,518–1,590
	,, 30th	1,600–1,670
	July 1st	1,680–1,800
	,, 2nd	1,760–1,945
	,, 8th	2,300–2,450
	,, 15th	1,930–1,990
	,, 22nd	2,210–2,250
	August 1st	2,690–3,010
	,, 8th	3,240–3,405
	,, 14th	3,540–3,780
	,, 15th	4,050–4,620

The causes of this catastrophic fall are not difficult to trace. Unfortunately discussion of these economic phenomena has been obscured by political bias, which has ascribed the fall to the deliberate design of the German Government, motived by the desire either to place an artificial premium on Germany's export trade, or to create a situation in which the plea of poverty could be put forward to secure a remission of reparation payments, or by both intentions. So far as the first intention is concerned, we have already disclosed the fallacies of the argument,[1] and it would be childish to suppose that the fallacies are not known to the German financial authorities. If a depreciating exchange were of lasting benefit to the export trade, we and every other nation should obviously set about depreciating our own currencies as fast as possible. As regards the second intention alleged, it is hard to believe that statesmen would put any hope in so transparent a manœuvre, still more difficult to

[1] See Chapter VII on the Balance of Trade.

believe that on such a slender chance of success they would risk plunging their own country into a social cataclysm. For that is what a continually depreciating currency brings in its train. By annihilating alike the savings of years and the highest rises in wages, it brings discontent to the point of revolution. What rising prices mean in the way of social difficulties we experienced in this country in 1919–20; and prices here rose slowly and steadily compared with what has been happening in Germany.

The idea that the depreciation of the mark has been deliberate is not only a priori too absurd to be believed by any intelligent person, but it is finally discredited by the actual historical sequence in which events occurred. There have been adequate and sufficient reasons for depreciation in the economic conditions obtaining.

In detail, the causes of this catastrophic fall are as follows: First, the Indemnity Policy imposed by the allied French and British Governments. The latter imposed the payment of large sums of money by way of indemnities from Germany, and as German currency was an altogether fluctuating quantity, and as most other European currencies were in a like condition, it was decided that Germany must pay the indemnity in one of two ways, either in gold or dollars. Now, of course, Germany had not the gold, and therefore it meant that Germany must buy dollars, and spend marks in buying them. The dollars which they bought were not used for the purpose of paying for imports into Germany, which would be manufactured up and sent out again, but were simply handed over to the Governments of France and England. That meant that on the foreign exchange market there was suddenly a huge influx of marks. The result was what is always the result when the supply of one commodity is suddenly increased in terms of another: the value of the mark went down.

The second cause is to be found in the decision of the Allies, promulgated in the autumn of 1921, to give a large portion of Upper Silesia to Poland. In the Germany of 1914 there were three great coalfields: the Saar Valley, the Ruhr Valley, and the Upper Silesian coalfield. Of these three, the Saar Valley had been previously transferred to France, the Ruhr Valley was partly occupied in providing large quantities of coal to France at a price far below the world-market price. The third was now handed over to Poland, together with a large portion of the industrial area of Upper Silesia. We have seen that the value of a country's currency to-day is based on what the country produces, or on its ability to produce at all. Taking away Upper Silesia reduced Germany's ability to produce, consequently the mark fell at once. The date on which the mark began its catastrophic fall in the autumn of 1921 coincided exactly with the date on which the news was received in Berlin that the decision in regard to Upper Silesia was going to be enforced.

The December, 1921, recovery of the mark was apparently due to hopes raised by the Washington Conference and by rumours of a credit to Germany to be arranged in London. The catastrophic fall from March, 1922, onward has been due to: (*a*) further far-reaching demands made by the Reparations Commission which involve foreign control over Germany's finances, control comparable to the kind exercised in Turkey; (*b*) the failure, owing to French opposition, of the negotiations for a loan; (*c*) the standing likelihood of French aggression against Germany's only remaining coalfield, the Ruhr Valley; (*d*) as a result of the continually rising prices, the instability of German political and social life. These conditions have lowered German credit still further and have deprived public opinion of any confidence in the financial future of the country. The indemnity policy and the taking away of mineral and agricultural land have had a continuous and cumulative effect; the economic position of Germany has become increasingly unsound and the mark increasingly weak. It is worthy of note that, as Mr. Keynes has pointed out, on occasion the increase in the note circulation has been not the cause but the effect of the decline in value of the mark. The order of causation has frequently been that political causes have sent down the value of the mark; the consequent rises in wages and prices have increased the German Government's expenses and rendered it unable to meet its short-term obligations (Treasury bills) as they mature; hence it has printed notes to meet the deficit.

Why, it may be asked, has not the activity of German workshops in 1920–22 redressed the balance? Because the German "boom" is far more illusory than the English boom of 1920. Up to August, 1922, Germany's trade balance has remained unfavourable. She is importing more than she is exporting. So many mineral and other resources have been taken away from her, the quantity of food and raw materials required to be imported is still so great,[1] that on the latest figures available her trade balance still shows a deficit, and this in spite of the limitation of consumption enforced on the mass of the German people. The confiscation of German shipping and oversea investments means that there are no "invisible exports" to offset this deficit, as is the case in England and was the case in Germany prior to the war. Germany, that is, in spite of her industrial activity, is not paying her way—altogether apart from reparations payments.

The indemnity, however, can ultimately be paid only in goods. If it is insisted that Germany pays in gold or

[1] The coal deliveries insisted on by France are so large that Germany, previously a coal-exporting country, has now, after losing the Saar and Silesian coalfields, to import coal and pay for it in foreign currency.

in dollars, she can only obtain them by selling goods to other countries. The payment of an indemnity implies, even apart from the devaluation of the mark, a surplus of exports, i.e. a big export trade. This, in turn, in a world whose buying power is diminished, implies unemployment elsewhere. But as, in spite of Germany's industrial activity, her exports do not provide a surplus over her imports, it follows that to buy the dollars insisted upon it is necessary to print notes to pay for them, and thus continually to diminish the value of the mark. The resulting artificial cheapening of German export prices provides an example of the limited benefit of a depreciating exchange.[1] If an English price in pounds and a German price in marks, quoted on Tuesday to a Dutch buyer, work out the same in florins, and on Thursday he finds he can get one-third more marks for his florins than he could on Tuesday, his price has been reduced by 33⅓ per cent., and in that case, of course, the quality of the article being equal, he buys the German goods. The price in German marks is the same, but the price to him has gone down. A market is thereby provided for German goods to the exclusion of others. At the same time the devaluation of the mark makes imports into Germany dearer, and thereby makes still more impossible the bridging of the gulf between imports and exports. German prices are always approximating upwards to world-prices, and sometimes reach them, as was the case, e.g. early in 1922, in the paper trade. But then some political cause causes the mark to depreciate and sets the whole process in motion again. The German economy is gripped by the jagged teeth of the vicious circle. It draws the British economy with it, and that in two ways:

First, Germany was before the war not only Britain's second largest customer, but also a large customer of many countries which in turn bought from Britain. A

[1] See Chapter VII.

Chilean nitrate exporter, a Brazilian coffee exporter, would employ the funds received from their sales to Hamburg in purchasing piece goods from Manchester. To-day, the devaluation of the mark has largely destroyed German purchasing power, and German imports have to be restricted to food and essential raw materials. She can buy neither from us. Our own oversea customers, who can no longer sell to Germany, are no longer able to buy from us.

Secondly, the volume of cheap exports which Germany sends out rests on the economic basis of low wages. The devaluation of the mark proceeds alike in terms of foreign currencies and in terms of commodities, though not to the same extent. Prices have risen to an enormous extent, wages and salaries to nothing like that extent. Real wages are far below what they were before the war; salaries, in terms of what they will buy, are at starvation rates. In June, 1922, prices had risen in the case of foodstuffs between 60 and 70 times the pre-war figures; in the case of clothing between 80 and 100 times. Wages had risen on an average about 25 times; the middle grade of salaries on an average between 15 and 18 times; higher salaries between 7 and 11 times; fixed incomes, of course, not at all.[1] The result is that wage-earners have a lower standard of life than before the war and the middle classes a very much lower standard, while middle-class people with small fixed incomes are destitute. Every further

[1] The above figures are quoted from an article by Mr. H. N. Brailsford in the "Nation" of July 15, 1922. They were originally given by the Prussian Premier to the Landtag, and their accuracy is, in Mr. Brailsford's experienced judgment, established by his own investigations. The present writer, who was himself in Germany at that time, is able to confirm them from his own investigation.

A bank clerk was then earning, in terms of what money would buy, roughly the equivalent of £1 per week; medium grade civil servants and commercial employees such as secretaries and accountants roughly one-quarter of the real remuneration they would receive in Britain.

step in the devaluation of the mark makes German exports cheaper, widens the gulf between imports and exports, confiscates savings, and reduces the real value of wages and salaries.

In all this there is nothing surprising. A considerable part of what has happened in regard to the mark exchange was prophesied by Professor Keynes in 1919.[1] Nor, even at that time, was he alone in his prophecy.

Whether the policy pursued by the peoples victorious in the Great War has been, on purely political grounds, a desirable one is not here in question. The subject of foreign exchange must deal largely with international economics, and students of it are compelled to furnish explanations of the phenomena they find. In doing so they cannot avoid temporary excursions into the dangerous No Man's Land which connects Economics with Politics, without thereby trespassing over the boundaries of the latter. It may, or may not, be the case that on other than economic grounds the policy pursued towards Germany is desirable or justifiable; there is no doubt that it has in fact caused the devaluation of the mark and the results therefrom above set out.

With the social effects of this catastrophic process, the extinguishing among large sections of the population of all opportunity for culture in the struggle to keep alive, it is impossible to deal here; but two attempts of the economic organism to adjust itself to a continually depreciating currency may be noticed. (1) Each fall in the mark has been accompanied by a rise in the value of industrial shares, because these shares represent property in fixed assets such as land, buildings, etc., which will not automatically lose their value with the next fall of the mark, as will, e.g., a bank deposit. This kind of investing is known as "the flight from the mark." (2) Soaring prices have led to great difficulty in financing

[1] "The Economic Consequences of the Peace."

business, and this difficulty has been only very partially met by increases in the capital of firms and limited companies. These increases represent merely a revaluation of assets in terms of the depreciated currency, and are not at all necessarily an indication of development work or increased prosperity. In fact, the returns obtained in many trades have been absurdly small. Dividends of hundreds per cent. in paper marks frequently shrivel down to 2 or 3 per cent. on the gold value of the capital invested in the business.

What will happen when, if at all, the mark stops depreciating and the stimulus to German exports of artificial cheapness is removed it is impossible to say.[1] Whether, under such circumstances, German trade will continue to be *konkurrenz-fahig,* i.e. capable of meeting foreign competition, is a subject of anxious debate amongst German economists. A long and painful period of economic and social readjustment would appear inevitable. What will happen if the mark does not stop depreciating it is also impossible to say. Other cases of currencies which have become worthless, such as those of Russia, Poland, and Austria, do not help us much, as these were not countries with a highly developed industrial organization. And if, finally, it is asked, "What is in fact likely to happen to the mark?" the answer is, "That depends on political considerations."[2] It is the burdens laid on Germany for political reasons—the occupation of the Rhineland, the deliveries of coal, the reparations payments—which are directly and primarily responsible for the increased note-issue in Germany and for the consequent devaluation of the mark.

[1] Apart, i.e., from the general considerations applying to such a case which are outlined in the next chapter.

[2] An answer the significance of which has been intensified by the events which have occurred since the above was written. The occupation of the Ruhr is a most striking example of the impossibility of separating finance from politics.

CHAPTER XIV

THE POST-WAR EXCHANGES

Continuation of inflation and depreciation after the war—Effect of war-finance on London Money Market—Floating debt—Effect of rises in bank rate under new conditions—New York as financial centre—Dollar rate from 1919 to 1922—Price deflation and monetary deflation—Possibility of a return to the gold standard—Deflation and a capital levy—Stabilization of the exchanges—Present position of British debt to U.S.A. and Allied debts to Britain—Conclusion.

OTHER post-war developments may be more briefly referred to. As soon as the artificial equilibrium of the war-period ended, the European currencies showed a rapid decline in terms of sterling, due in the first instance to the necessity of paying for the replenishment of stocks. Despite the general postponement in 1919 of the payment of interest on war debts owed by continental nations to Britain, these currencies continued to be inflated, and consequently to depreciate, a tendency which has been intensified by political instability on the Continent. Of the Central and East European currencies, the only one which attained a fair measure of stability, due to the cessation of inflation, was that of Czecho-Slovakia, where the krone remained fairly steady. The Austrian krone and the Polish mark became, like the Russian rouble, practically worthless. The Scandinavian and Dutch currencies were unfavourably affected by trade conditions in Russia and Germany respectively, that of Norway being particularly affected by the slump in shipping freights during and after 1920.

The rates reflect the utter disorganization of European economic life by the war. The resources of Britain have not nearly sufficed for the work of reconstruction. During the boom of June, 1919, to June, 1920, considerable quantities of goods were supplied by Britain to the Continent on credit. But as our imports of food and raw material from the Western Hemisphere had to be paid for in cash, this method of doing business was felt to be dangerous, and came to an end after the making of credit dearer which was caused by the raising of bank rate in November, 1919, and April, 1920.

On the working of the London Money Market, the effect of the process of inflation described in Chapter XI has been to cause the market to be dominated by the requirements of Government finance. The most important factor in it has been the Floating Debt. The Floating Debt is that portion of the Government debt which is held by the money market, and it consisted in the main of two items: (1) Ways and Means Advances, i.e. the Government's overdraft at the Bank of England, and advances by Public Departments, and (2) Treasury Bills. Treasury bills are in effect promises by the Government to pay, of £1,000 each, which mature in 3, 6, 9, or 12 months from the date of issue. The reason why the money market to-day is dominated by the Treasury bill issue is that it knows that if the holders of Treasury bills do not renew them when they become due, the Government, in order to repay them, will be forced to increase its overdraft at the Bank of England, i.e. to borrow on ways and means advances. Such borrowing will inflate credit, and hence currency, in the manner already described, so that although money may be tight at the minute, it is bound to become easier. Tightness of money in the money market means that people will insist on having their Treasury bills repaid when they become due: that implies that the Government will have to borrow on ways and means advances, and that in turn means further inflation and the consequent relative easiness of money. In other words, tightness of money will automatically bring easiness of money. The whole position revolves around the quantity of Treasury bills in existence. The demand on the part of trade for accommodation from the market does not weigh on the position so heavily as do the requirements of the Government.

Formerly, people who operated in the money market looked to the Bank of England's weekly return to inform them of the position. The item of private deposits in that return showed how much money there was in the market, and the ratio of the reserve to liabilities, frequently referred to in the financial columns of the Press as "the ratio," showed how far it was safe to go in the creation of credit, and therefore how far the banks were likely to go in creating it. To-day, the money market knows that if Treasury bills are not renewed, credit will be automatically created. The whole money market position is dominated by the Treasury bill issue. That in turn is the ultimate reason why the raising of the bank rate to-day does not produce the effect on the exchanges which it used to do before the war. It will be remembered that its effect was produced by the restriction of the volume of credit in existence, and thereby the making of what remained more valuable. To-day the raising of bank rate cannot restrict the volume of credit in existence to the necessary extent or permanently, because making money tight will be automatically followed by Government borrowing on ways and means, which will make it easier again. So long as these conditions exist, the raising of bank rate is inoperative to limit the creation of credit, and therefore inoperative to turn the exchanges in our favour. That statement is subject of course to this limitation: rises in the bank rate such as we had in November, 1919, and April, 1920, do produce higher interest rates all round, and to that extent do check speculation and limit the creation of commercial credit. There is good reason to suppose that the beginning of the end of the speculative price boom of 1919–20 was caused by the increase in the bank rate in April, 1920. The point however is that the requirements of the Government are so large compared to the requirements of the ordinary commercial trader, that the amount of limitation which the raising of the bank rate can enforce is nothing like sufficient to produce any appreciable effect on the total volume of credit, and therefore on the volume of our currency. The raising of the bank rate in 1920 was probably justified in that it tended to eliminate the speculative element which was forcing prices up to dangerous heights. But it did not, could not, and was not expected to produce the effect on the foreign exchanges which before the war it would have produced. London no longer holds the position as the centre of international finance which it held before the war. It enjoys a primacy in Europe greater than before the war, and it has been frequently the case that payments due from continental countries to the United States have been made through London. But London is no longer a free gold market,[1] whereas New York is: a sterling bill is not, whereas a dollar bill is, a claim to gold which can be always enforced. No occasion has arisen since the war when gold could not be obtained in New York. The change compared with the conditions which obtained in 1907 is due to (*a*) the reorganization of the U.S. banking system following 1907 by the institution of the Federal Reserve Bank, and (*b*) the effect of the war in concentrating a large part of the world's available gold

[1] See Chapter II.

supply in New York. Theoretically, it might have been expected that the dollar bill would, in international acceptance business of the kind exemplified in Chapter IV, have entirely superseded the sterling bill. In fact, while the vogue of the dollar bill has very greatly increased, the two continue to exist side by side. The reason is that currency factors, like all other economic factors, take time to produce their full effect. Moreover, there are other considerations involved. Custom and prestige play a great part in commerce as in other things. London, having had a long experience of this class of business, knows the ropes in a way that it is quite impossible for New York or any other centre to learn in the course of a few years. New York bankers have frequently been urged since the war to go in more for this class of business, which the financial position of New York renders them eminently able to do, but up to the present they have suffered from the very natural fault of over-caution. They had a big shake-up in the financial crisis in 1907; and, although the U.S. banking system is much securer now than it was then, the conditions of European trade since the war have not been inviting. It is easy to understand the unwillingness which has been evident in New York to extend the credit which is necessary if they are going to do this business. In the present state of Europe, and in fact of the whole world, the position of a relatively inexperienced banking community, such as is the New York banking community relatively to that of London, has been very difficult. When things settle down, it is probable that the accepting and international banking business of New York will increase steadily, especially in those regions of the world in which America is more particularly interested, i.e. South America, the Caribbean Sea, and the Far East, as well as Canada.

The loss by London of pre-eminence in finance, its

connexion with exchange questions, and its results on international trade are excellently illustrated by the following letter which was written in 1920 by the American representative of a firm of cotton brokers in Liverpool to his principals :—

"Before the war, Liverpool, as the largest consuming market in the world, set the price, and especially the basis for the sale of cotton to the whole of Europe—that is to say, about seven to eight million bales of American cotton were sold every season, based on Liverpool futures. This was largely due to the fact that London financed all these sales of cotton to continental markets. London was the banking centre of the world, and understood European finance far better than any New York banks. Further, even in America, if a shipper in the South wanted to know what cotton was really worth, he would take the Liverpool prices and calculate from them what he could afford to pay for the purchase of his cotton.

"Since the war this situation has changed entirely. The varying rate of sterling exchange has made it impossible for continental spinners to buy based on Liverpool futures, and now the whole of the business to France, Germany, Italy, Spain, as well as Japan, etc., is all based on New York futures. London is no longer the financial centre of the world, although it is still quite evident that the bankers there understand European financing better than it is understood in New York. Nevertheless, cotton shipped to continental markets is now paid for cash in New York. Continental spinners, if they now want credit, turn to New York, and not to London, and it still remains to be seen if London will ever be able to regain its financial supremacy."

To the fact that London is no longer a free gold market

is to be ascribed the tendency for oversea enterprises and foreign loans which would formerly have been financed in London to be floated in New York. So far as giving New York the financial primacy of the Western Hemisphere is concerned, the war has hastened by some decades the development which would probably have taken place slowly during the twentieth century. New York has not so far, however, played the part in financing European reconstruction which was expected early in 1919.[1] This is due partly to the fact that time is required to educate the American investor up to the export of capital, chiefly to the disturbed political conditions of Europe, which involve capital invested in risks which it will not face while safer opportunities obtain elsewhere, e.g. South America and the Far East. The existing world primacy of New York, however, is demonstrated by the fact that the main course of money rates in London follows that in New York Bank rate itself since 1919 has followed the re-discount rate of the Federal Reserve Bank, and the discount houses habitually "watch New York."

The course of the London-New York rate is particularly interesting. After the unpegging of the dollar exchange in March, 1919, sterling declined rapidly in value, despite the postponement for three years of all interest payments on Britain's debts to the U.S. Sterling in New York at one time went as low as 3·12, and after remaining between 3·50 and 3·90 during 1920, rose somewhat in 1921 and considerably in 1922. That sterling should be higher in 1921 and 1922, years of trade depression, than during the boom of 1920 is explicable by three considerations: (*a*) Although it is correct in terms of post-war conditions to call 1920 a "boom" year, the trade figures for 1920, when recalculated in terms of 1913 prices, were far below

[1] This expectation was widely held not only in London but, as the writer can from personal experience testify, in New York as well.

1913 figures. The volume of exports in 1920, compared with 1913 figures, so far from justifying the term " boom," were far below the pre-war average. The 1919–20 " boom " was solely a price boom, in which the U.S. and other countries participated, which could not therefore turn the balance of trade sufficiently in our favour to raise the value of sterling in terms of the dollar. (*b*) While the " boom " continued, imports of raw material were made on a large scale on the assumption that it would continue for an indefinite period; these imports were mainly paid for in cash. A good deal of our exports during this period, on the other hand, were made on a credit basis. The raw material came to a large extent from the Western Hemisphere, and dollars had to be bought to pay for it; whereas to the extent to which British merchants extended credit abroad a corresponding demand for sterling did not of course come into existence. (*c*) The decline in prices during 1921–22 was greater in Britain than in the U.S. During the latter portion of the period, in fact, prices in the U.S. were again rising, i.e. the dollar was losing in value. The continued drop in prices in Britain was simultaneously increasing the value of the pound sterling. Sterling during this period therefore gained more in value than did the dollar—we are speaking of rates of improvement, of course, not of absolute values—and accordingly its value in terms of the dollar went up.

The same causes which raised the dollar value of the pound sterling concurrently increased its gold value.

This process of price deflation has thrown into the background the question of direct monetary deflation dealt with by the Cunliffe Committee in 1918–19. That Committee made certain recommendations which amounted to a gradual calling in and cancelling of currency notes until the pound sterling had been brought to its par value as measured by the dollar exchange.

Their recommendations amounted, in other words, to a policy of gradual monetary deflation. That policy was not carried out to the extent to which its more convinced advocates thought desirable. The calling in and cancelling of currency notes until the paper pound is on a parity with the gold pound could only have been accomplished if the Government had had at its command sufficient funds, i.e. if there had been a sufficient surplus

Date	Amount of Currency Note Issue (in million pounds)	Gold (Coin and Bullion) held against Currency Notes (in million pounds)
Dec. 30th, 1914	38	18½
„ „ 1915	103	28½
„ „ 1916	150	28½
„ „ 1917	212	28½
„ „ 1918	323	28½
June 25th, 1919	342	28½
Dec. 31st, 1919	356	28½
„ 29th, 1920	364	28½
„ 28th, 1921	323	28½
Mar. 29th, 1922	298	28½
June 28th, 1922	294	28½
Dec. 27th, 1922	300	27

of income over expenditure. Apart from that, of which there was no sign, monetary deflation was impossible. The main lines of the Committee's policy were however adopted, in particular the limitation of the fiduciary circulation of currency notes (i.e. that portion not backed by gold or by Bank of England notes). But the main element in deflation has been the price deflation referred to above.

Price deflation has been accompanied by a reduction

in the volume of the Floating Debt, which during the year 1922 lowered its total from approximately £1,300,000,000 to approximately £950,000,000. A lower Floating Debt indicates that less circulating currency is being required. The price deflation and the concurrent reduction of the Floating Debt have accordingly enabled the volume of the currency note issued to be reduced in the manner indicated by the table shown on page 176. Without some such reduction the increase in value of the pound sterling in terms of the dollar could not have been achieved.[1]

The rise in the value of sterling has raised discussion on the possibility of a definite return to the gold standard. It is understood that it is only in Britain, Holland, and Scandinavia that this question can become a practical one. The French, Italian, Central and East European currencies have become devaluated to such an extent that a return to the gold standard does not come into question. So far as Britain is concerned, the possibility of such a return depends on the answer to the question how far the rise that has taken place is likely to be permanent. This deflation, we have seen, has been in the nature of price deflation, and is partly the result of allowing stocks of imported material to run down. In the event of any considerable revival in trade, the building up of stocks would become necessary and prices would rise. More money would be required by trade. The rate of discount and the rate of interest for loans and overdrafts would rise, and here, it seems, would be felt the fatal weakness of the Floating Debt. Holders of Treasury bills, finding a more remunerative use for their money, would fail to renew them; and the Government would have to borrow on ways and means advances. In other words, the process of inflation would recommence; prices

[1] See Chapter XI.

would rise faster in Britain than in the U.S. by reason of this element of inflation, and the benefits of price deflation would partly be lost. The crux of the whole position is the Floating Debt. If the aim be a permanent return to the gold standard, it is essential that the Treasury bill position should cease to dominate the money market; in other words, that the Government's requirements should be further reduced. The difficulty of the situation is increased by the fact of a declining revenue and an expenditure many items of which are fixed. But evidently, if the price deflation which has occurred is to be permanent, public economy is as necessary as it would have been to monetary deflation pure and simple.

As the possibility of a return to the gold standard bulks so largely in exchange problems and affects profoundly the future financial status of London, it seems justifiable to indicate very briefly the general questions of financial policy which deflation has raised.

Deflation has been strongly attacked by some of the industrialists of this country, who argued that although deflation means a more favourable exchange, it means also, which is true, that foreign countries whose currencies have depreciated still more than ours will be less able to buy our goods than they were previously, and will be able to undersell us in other markets. That is obviously a very *ex parte* argument. To criticize it in detail here is unnecessary, as we have already examined the fallacy of the argument that a depreciated currency benefits the export trade.[1] The increases in the price of imported food and raw material, which depreciating the currency would necessarily imply, would be particularly disastrous to Britain, which depends so largely for her supplies of both on imports. This is hardly the time to increase costs of raw material and

[1] See Chapter VII.

labour, to send up the costs of living, and create friction between employer and employed, or to follow Germany downhill.[1] Deflation implies cheaper food, cheaper manufacturing costs, and—above all—an increased credit power to finance foreign trade. The importance of the last consideration cannot be exaggerated from the point of view of taking the lead in the reconstruction of Europe, with the benefits to this country which that leadership would imply.

The same fallacy underlies the argument that deflation is responsible for unemployment. If deflation has rendered it more difficult for countries with depreciated currencies to buy our goods, the fall in prices made possible by decreased costs of labour and raw material has rendered it easier. The reason for the existing unemployment is the general exhaustion of the world's purchasing power, owing to the destruction of wealth during the war. The "boom" of 1919–20 was only an interlude, due in the first instance to the necessity for replacing stocks and the desire to spend profits made during the war; then the rise in prices led to speculative activity. If this activity had not been checked by rises in the bank rate, there would have been many more failures in the liquidation of the following years. For when the war-profits were spent and the stocks replaced, the "boom" had to come to an end. The purchasing power necessary to sustain a flourishing export trade did not and does not exist; it was destroyed between 1914 and 1918. The number of our unemployed corresponds roughly to the increase in population since 1913, and this "high" figure of unemployment—"high" compared with pre-war times—is probably one of the "normal" features of the post-war era. It is true that in Germany a depreciating currency has temporarily stimulated exports and resulted in a very small degree of unemploy-

[1] See Chapter XIII.

ment. But—apart from the instability of the situation in Germany—the small degree of unemployment is only possible by reason of the fact that the great mass of Germans have, unwillingly or willingly, accepted a very much lower standard of life than before the war. In England, on the contrary, many classes of the population are enjoying about the same standard as in 1914. That large numbers of others are unemployed is the corollary of this. The pound and the mark illustrate the error of supposing that a long war need not be paid for by the mass of the population, if only you know how to juggle with currencies and prices. Industrial nations, depending on exports for their livelihood, are left to choose between the total impoverishment of some and the partial impoverishment of all.

The only means whereby this state of affairs can be ameliorated is the establishment abroad of conditions under which the European countries and their overseas customers can gradually recover their purchasing power.

A further consideration in favour of the policy of deflation until the gold standard is restored is the fact that the interest on our debt to the U.S. and repayments of the principal thereof have to be paid in dollars.[1] The more dollars sterling will purchase, the less the burden of the debt becomes. It is of course true that ultimately this debt, like Reparations, can only be paid in goods. But depreciation tends, as we have seen,[2] to bring about a gap between purchasing power parity and exchange rates, and the burden of the debt would be heavier by the extent of this gap. Moreover the benefits of a depreciating exchange are pocketed by certain classes of the population, while the ill effects are felt by the national exchequer, especially when it has to buy foreign currencies; and no practicable system of taxation has yet

[1] See below, p. 185.

[2] See Chapter XII, especially p. 148.

been discovered whereby the national revenue can be secured against the losses due to a depreciating currency. In the case of an appreciating currency, on the other hand, the national revenue benefits, since takes are worth more, in terms of goods and dollars, when they are collected than when they were imposed, while the loss falls on those who hold stocks, i.e. on the same people, in the main, who benefited previoously when the currency declined.

The British Treasury's persistence in the policy of gradual deflation in face of the opposition of those, standing politically on both the Right and the Left, who would have benefited by a continuance of inflation, in a case in which the Civil Service was able to protect the long-period interests od the State against the ephemeral interests of groups.

Deflation, again, is frequently objected to on the ground that it makes the burden of internal war debt heavier. It is easier, it is argued, to pay these debts in a depreciated currency than in one restored to its former value. The problem is complicated by the fact that these debts were incurred at different levels of money values and that the stock frequently changes hands. The difficulty is not met by the proposal to scale down the interest on war loans, which appears to discriminate against this class of security. Advocates of deflation must, it seems, be prepared to face the fact that the procedure they advocate may necessitate a general capital levy in order to reduce the burden of the war debt. The desirability or otherwise of a capital levy is a matter of the economics of taxation, and cannot be discussed here. But it may be pointed out that in principle there is no difference between a capital levy and the income tax.

We may broadly sum up the effects of the war on the exchanges somewhat as follows: (1) The war itself and the political and economic reactions set up by it have destroyed so much wealth that the currencies of all the European nations which took part in it, and to some extent of those which did not, have lost value in different degrees. As regards the belligerent countries, this effect is most marked in Russia, and least marked in Britain. The means whereby the destruction of values has expressed itself in currency values is inflation, but the fundamental cause of the devaluation of the currencies is the destruction alike of wealth, confidence, and credit. Apart from the possible case of Britain and certain small "neutral" countries, therefore, there can be no question of a return to Mint Par, i.e. pre-war values, until the destruction has been made good, i.e. not for an indefinite period. (2) As the destruction has taken place in different degrees, the equilibrium of pre-war times has been upset. Hence the currencies are not only depreciated in value but also wildly fluctuating.

The obvious theoretical remedy is to stabilize the exchanges, i.e. to make them exchangeable against gold at fixed rates, the rates chosen being such as they can reasonably be expected to maintain. If such a plan could be carried into effect it would restore a measure of certainty to exchange movements. And one technical objection brought against it, based on the difference between the internal and the external value of a depreciated currency such as the mark, does not seem vital, as it appears unlikely that, if stabilization could once be accomplished, this difference would be more than temporary.[1]

Stabilization would bring us face to face with the issue raised at the end of Chapter VII: given a country with a depreciated currency, and supposing that the process of depreciating comes to an end, by reason of the fact that the internal and external influences which have been adversely affecting the currency cease to be operative,

[1] See Chapters VII and XII.

what will happen to its exchange rates? Suppose, e.g. that a practicable arrangement about reparations and war-debts repayments were made, a political equilibrium established in Europe and recourse to inflation ceased—conditions which as we shall see later are in fact an indispensable preliminary to the settlement of Europe —what would happen to the depreciated European currencies?

In the first place, as regards the exchange value of such a currency at the time when the adverse influences cease to be operative, it is probable that where the past inflation has been considerable, the exchange value will for some time be less than purchasing power parity, by reason of the secondary effect of inflation in lowering the credit of the issuing country. In so far as the loss of exchange value is due to the discounting of a supposedly unfavourable future, it may be expected to be recovered when the adverse influences cease to be operative. As regards prices, it is likely that the effects of past inflation will require some time to work themselves out. The probability is, therefore, that even after exchange values have recovered somewhat, there will still remain a gap between them and purchasing power parity. But two forces will be at work to close it. On the one hand, prices will be moving upwards towards a new level determined by the extent of past inflation, the supply of commodities available, and the velocity of circulation of the currency. On the other hand, the fact that exchange values are lower than purchasing power parity will, as we have seen earlier, enable exporters for some time longer to undersell their rivals abroad. The resulting export boom will, other things being equal and in the absence of further inflation, create abroad a demand for the currency in question in order to pay for these goods, and this demand will send up the exchange value of the currency. These two forces will, in the absence of other disturbing factors, tend to close up the gap between the internal and the external value of the currency. As the two values approach one another, the export boom will slacken, for the rise in prices will pull wages and salaries after it, and costs of production will rise; exporters will have continually to revise their price lists upwards. Finally, when exchange rates approximate to purchasing power parity, the two processes will stop. For on the one hand, there will be no further inducement for the prices of the goods entering into international trade to rise, since they have reached the level of world-prices; while on the other, the exchange value of the currency will no longer tend to appreciate, since export prices will no longer be artificially cheap to foreigners. What remains of the export boom will die away and be replaced by competition on a more or less equal footing. The general level of home prices may perhaps take a little longer to adjust itself to the new equilibrium; and the difficulties which usually follow a boom might be expected to make their appearance: liquidations, unemployment, and unrest. From this stage of more or less normal competition onward, exchange rates will fluctuate within relatively narrow limits round purchasing power parity. In the absence of some new disturbing factor, such as fresh inflation, large reparations or war-debts repayments, or political events, the balance of trade and interest payments will rule exchange rates, perhaps keeping rates and purchasing power parity steady, perhaps causing them to move slowly together in one direction or the other. In either case the direction would depend on such factors as the nature of the political settlement and the debt settlement, natural advantages, standards of life, real wages, and the productivity of labour; it would no longer be primarily a currency question.

Assuming stabilization to be desirable, the practical

difficulties in the way are enormous. Clearly two conditions are essential to any scheme of stabilization: (1) The general cessation of inflation, and (2) a general arrangement in regard to international indebtedness. Both conditions are essential, and both are very difficult to establish in practice.

The difficulties in the way of the first are (*a*) the governmental extravagance which is a result of war psychology and war habits; (*b*) the demand of the peoples who have been through the war for governmental easing of their burdens, and in particular their refusal, especially in France, to submit to the taxation necessary to put their finances on a sound footing; (*c*) in the case of Germany, the reparations demands, which made inflation inevitable—there is no alternative here to inflation on the one hand or a drastic scaling-down of reparations on the other.

The difficulties in the way of a general arrangement in regard to international indebtedness are no less. The position is as follows: Britain owes the U.S. a sum in dollars equivalent, at par, to £978,000,000. She is owed a somewhat larger amount by her former Allies and Dominions. Germany owes an indefinite sum in respect of reparations. The suggestion that the U.S. should take over the Allied debt to Britain, or the reparations liability of Germany, in satisfaction or part satisfaction of the British debt to the U.S., has been rejected. Of the £978,000,000 referred to, £851,000,000 represent the capital sum borrowed during the war and £127,000,000 the interest accrued between 1919 and 1922, during which period interest was not paid but added to the principal. Britain is now committed to yearly payments of interest at 3 per cent. for the first ten years from 1923 onwards, and 3½ per cent. afterwards until the debt is finally cleared off by the operation of a sinking fund of a half per cent. per annum. As regards the debt owed to Britain by her Allies, no payments of interest have so far been made, let alone any repayment of the principal. It is well known that the European debtors of Britain are in the main unwilling or unable to pay interest, and the French Government has made a public declaration to this effect. The attitude of the British Government, as represented by the Balfour Note of 1922, was that Britain was willing to consider favourably a general writing down of international debts, as between the U.S. and Britain, Britain and her debtors, and the recently allied Powers and Germany; but that failing such a general writing-down, Britain would be compelled to look to her debtors for settlement to the extent to which she was herself pressed for payment by the U.S. There have been suggestions that this attitude may be susceptible of modification, at any rate so far as regards the writing-down of debt between Britain and her recent Allies on the one hand and the Allies and Germany on the other.

The core of the exchange situation is the devaluation of the mark and the economic position of Germany. Eastern Europe before the war was largely dependent on German industry and finance, and its reconstruction to-day is similarly dependent. On its reconstruction depends the utilization of its agricultural and mineral resources, for which the industrial peoples of Western Europe are now dependent to a great extent on the Western Hemisphere, and also its restoration as a market for industrial products. On the restoration of the buying power of Germany, again, depends a great portion of the prosperity of both Europe and such oversea markets as Chili, Brazil, and the Argentine. Before the war, these countries sold largely to Germany, and bought largely from Britain. To-day, their inability to do the first contributes largely to their inability to do the second. Lastly, Germany herself was, formerly, next to India, Britain's best customer. All these matters are inextricably bound up with the devaluation of the mark. The chairman of the Norddeutscher Lloyd was not talking nonsense when he said early in 1919, "If Britain fears her interests will be damaged by the fall of the mark, her best plan is to help to raise its value."

But this raises the whole set of problems. In discussing the possibility of stabilizing the exchanges, we used the words "general cessation of inflation," "general arrangement in regard to international indebtedness." Any scheme of stabilization or deflation which is more than the substitution of one kind of paper for another, any scheme which would really make possible the return of Europe to economic health, depends on the prior settlement of reparations and "inter-Allied" indebtedness. Such an agreement implies, not merely an agreement between experts on matters of technical finance, but an agreement between democratic peoples on matters of fundamental interest. The period following the close of the Great War is the most difficult period that could be imagined in which to secure general agreement between the peoples who were fighting. Financial problems are ultimately political problems. It is safe to say, however—whatever may be the desirability or possibility on political grounds of some measure of European agreement to restore order, stability, and mutual help—that without it there appears no reason why the economic situation of Europe should improve, and no reason therefore why the exchanges should not continue along the path they have followed since 1919.[1]

[1] Since the above was written, the Franco-Belgian occupation of the Ruhr has deprived the mark of all value; the franc and lira have also declined, indicating the worsening of the general economic situation.

BIBLIOGRAPHY FOR STUDENTS

GENERAL

SPALDING: "Foreign Exchange and Foreign Bills."
CLARE: "A B C of the Foreign Exchanges."
„ "Primer of the Money Market."
HARTLEY WITHERS: "The Meaning of Money."
„ „ "Money Changing."
GOSCHEN: "The Foreign Exchanges."
ESCHER: "Elements of Foreign Exchange."
SYKES: "Banking and Currency" (Chapters XIX to XXII).

THE EXCHANGES AT THE OUTBREAK OF WAR

HARTLEY WITHERS: "The War and Lombard Street."

BILLS OF EXCHANGE

The Bills of Exchange Act, 1882.
WHITTAKER: "Foreign Exchange."

THE EASTERN EXCHANGES

SPALDING: "Eastern Exchange, Currency, and Finance."
Article in "The Times Trade Supplement" of February 7, 1920.

INFLATION

RIGHT HON. R. MCKENNA: Speech at the Annual Meeting of the London Joint City and Midland Bank, reported in weekly Press of January 31, 1920.

Final and Interim Reports of the Cunliffe Committee (H.M. Stationery Office).

PROF. E. CANNAN: Articles in "Manchester Guardian" of January 30 and 31, 1920, entitled *Paper Money and Prices.*

PROF. E. CANNAN: "The Paper Pound of 1797 to 1819."

HARTLEY WITHERS: "War-Time Financial Problems" (Chapters III, IV, XVI, XVIII).

GIBSON: "British Finance During and After the War."

INTERNATIONAL INDEBTEDNESS

KEYNES: "The Economic Consequences of the Peace."

" "A Revision of the Treaty."

"Manchester Guardian" Commercial Reconstruction Number 2.

PURCHASING POWER PARITY

"Manchester Guardian" Commercial Reconstruction Number 1: Article by Prof. Keynes and authorities there quoted.

GREGORY: "The Foreign Exchanges Before, During and After the War."

STABILIZATION OF THE EXCHANGES

"Manchester Guardian" Commercial Reconstruction Number 1: Articles by Prof. Keynes and Dr. Melchior, etc.

INDEX